How to
Clean
Practically
Anything

2nd edition

How to Clean Practically Anything

2nd edition

SYDNEY PEMBERTON

CHOICEBOOKS

CHOICEBOOKS

Copyright © Sydney Pemberton 1997, 2004

First published in 1997
Reprinted 1997, 1998
Second edition published in 2004 by
CHOICE BOOKS
57 Carrington Road Marrickville 2204 Australia

National Library of Australia
Cataloguing-in-publication data

Pemberton, Syd.
    How to clean practically anything.
    2nd ed.
    Includes index.
    ISBN 1 920705 24 4.

    1. Cleaning. 2. House cleaning. I. Title.

648.5

Designed and illustrated by Deborah Parry Graphics

Typeset in house by CHOICE BOOKS
Cover design and illustration Deborah Parry Graphics

Printed in Australia by Southwood Press

CONTENTS

INTRODUCTION

I n this so-called modern world no magic all-purpose vacuum cleaner or feather duster has been invented to deal with the cleaning jobs with one supersonic suck or flick. What we have instead are rows of supermarket shelves packed with a huge variety of cleaning products, which, it is claimed, will save us time and elbow grease We, of course, gain more leisure time to enjoy our shining home and the environment around us. The selection of products on offer can be confusing, and if we actually bought a special cleaner for each household chore, we might need a whole room in which to store them.

The precious and fragile environment we live in, however, should make us consider what is in these wonder products and choose less environmentally harmful cleaning products and practices. There are often alternative products we can consider if we really wish to reduce the growing problem of allergies, pollution of our waterways and ever increasing cost of the damage to our environment.

In days gone by, of course, grand houses had a butler's pantry or scullery where the butler and housekeeper polished and cleaned everything in sight, and maids and menservants galore to sweep and wash and clean. Even not-so-grand households often had a specialist cleaner or a washing lady who came in once a week to 'do'. Times have changed and most of us now have to do it ourselves, often without expert knowledge to help us work out what cleaning tactic to use for particular problems, such as very tarnished silver.

This book intends to be a comprehensive guide to help you with everyday cleaning tasks and the maintenance and care of more unusual objects inside or outside the house. We all have to clean something at some time in our lives. Our home reflects the lifestyle and personality of the people who inhabit it. The things we gather around us in our nest are an extension of who we are. I hope this book will encourage and inspire the care and maintenance of things familiar and precious which in turn will add to the comfort and ambience of that place called 'home'. After all, there is no place like it!

Cleaning should also include taking care of the environment. I believe we have to look after our planet and care not only for our immediate environment, which is our home, but also the wider environment of community and of course the world. As consumers, we need to be aware of waste, inappropriate or excessive packaging, recycling, composting and using chemicals that have the least impact on the environment.

Understanding what is in a product begins with the labelling. Many products these days list what the product is made of and how it should be used and disposed of. Recognising symbols and codes on labelling can sometimes be difficult, so look for detergents that carry the Australian Standard for biodegradability (AS 4351) or International Standard (ISO 7827), as well as phosphate-free detergents, where possible.

In Australia, it is mandatory for refrigerators, freezers, clothes washers, clothes dryers, dishwashers and airconditioners to carry a label rating the energy efficiency of the appliance—the more stars, the better efficiency. Functions like economy wash for dishwashers and washing machines earn a product stars. Water, being our most precious resource, needs to be saved where possible, so appliances and equipment that cut down on the use of water should be considered when it comes time to replace them.

Local councils and Water Board information centres will supply information on water-tanks and the use of grey water from the home. The upside of investing in any of these changes in the home can mean savings on household bills!

Chapter 1

THE ORGANISED CLEANER

S easonal changes will have us dragging out household goods and clothing to accommodate rising or falling temperatures. The bright glare of spring sunlight streaming into the home and highlighting every dusty spot, may encourage us to start a cleaning frenzy, but spring is not the only season to have a good clean. 'Little and often' is a good motto to keep on top of the jobs at hand, and the big cleaning jobs can be spread throughout the year.

If the following program does not fit into your schedule, plan your own and set it up somewhere handy so you (and your family) can refer to it easily. You don't have to do all the jobs yourself, and some might need the skills of a professional cleaning company. The days of sending a small ragged person up the chimney with a wire brush are over— these days chimney sweeps arrive with an electric vacuum and soft brushes.

A Cleaning Calendar

THE DAILY ROUTINE

Wipe down all used kitchen surfaces—cooktop, oven, grill (if used), benchtops, splashback, microwave, sink

Clean all dishes—load or unload the dishwater

Empty the drainer—put dishes away

Clean pets' bowls

Wipe down all bathroom surfaces after use—bath, shower, toilet, washbasin, and mop floor

Tidy living area

Make beds

Put away clothes—in wardrobe or chest of drawers or dirty linen box

Empty kitchen compost and rubbish bins to outside bins

Scoop leaves from the swimming pool

If you can do only half the things on this list, you are doing well. Kitchens and bathrooms are the most important—the rest of the mess you can shut the door on!

Try to delegate some of the jobs to other household members so that it is a co-operative effort. Rotate the jobs so that everyone has a go at different household skills.

THE WEEKLY ROUTINE

Dust every room that is in use

Vacuum, sweep or mop main traffic areas

Air all rooms—open up a few windows

Thoroughly clean stove top and rangehood

Wipe fronts of kitchen cupboards and built-in appliances

Wipe over the outside of the fridge, washing machine and drier

Sweep kitchen and bathroom and clean with a mop

Sweep and remove dust and leaves from all entrances to the home and beat dust out of doormats

Empty bins and wash and disinfect kitchen and bathroom rubbish bins—put out household garbage and recycled rubbish where applicable

Change bed linen

Laundry—soak, wash, dry and iron*

Clean out pets' cages, bedding, hutch or run

Scrub any algae from the swimming pool walls

*If there is a lot of washing to do, spread it out over the week. Small hand or machine washes every other day (as long as you do full loads) are better than one mighty one. Spending a few minutes each day hanging out or taking in a small wash is better than having to spend perhaps an hour hanging out a large wash, then taking it in, sorting and folding it. Ironing can be done while you catch up with your favourite television or radio program or listen to a CD.

A Cleaning Calendar

THE FORTNIGHTLY ROUTINE

Vacuum under furniture and dust or vacuum clean upholstered furniture in the most frequently used rooms

Wipe over the outside and inside of the oven

Clean out the fridge—get rid of food that has passed its used-by date

These little jobs will make the workload less when it comes to a thorough clean once a month. The fridge is always a good indication of how many meals you have cooked at home, what take-aways you have had or if you have been out to eat.

THE MONTHLY ROUTINE

Clean mirrors and picture frames

Clean one room thoroughly—wipe down woodwork and doors, vacuum curtains, clean blinds, polish metals, wash or dust ornaments

Turn the mattresses in each bedroom

Air bedding and hang pillows and doonas outside in the sun (if possible)

Sharpen all kitchen knives if blunt

Clean the car if necessary inside and out

Clean more than one room if you have time and if you feel it needs it. If you do not have a car, clean your bike or motorbike or all your walking shoes.

THE QUARTERLY ROUTINE

Clean windows in the most frequently used rooms

Polish wooden furniture and floors if necessary

Clean the pantry cupboards and make a shopping list

Defrost the fridge and clean out the freezer—remove food that has passed its use-by date

Wipe and clean all electrical equipment—television, computer, CD player, DVD or VCR, telephone, fax and answering machine

Wash cleaning equipment—brooms, mops, cloths if they are reuseable, dishwasher, washing machine, vacuum cleaner

Clean out one cupboard or drawer and sort through any accumulated junk

Clean out fireplace thoroughly and/or air-conditioning filters and extractor fans

Tidy shed, garage or veranda

Take the car to have it serviced if necessary

The thing about quarterly sorting out and cleaning is that if your electrical equipment needs mending or servicing this will remind you to do it. It will also keep you in touch with what you should be eating from your freezer before it has to be thrown away. All of this is helpful and might save you some money.

A Cleaning Calendar

THE YEARLY ROUTINE

Shampoo or deep clean rugs and carpets

Clean upholstered furniture

Take down curtains and wash or dry-clean

Clean light fittings

Call in the chimney sweep

Clean out guttering and check drains

Clean out wardrobes and chests of drawers and put away seasonal clothes

Clean bookshelves and dust and re-sort books

Recycle or pass on or throw out any completely useless things or clothes in the 'this could come in handy' category which have been stored for too long

Service electric blankets

Clean the backs of cupboards and the fridge and behind pictures and mirrors

Oil, clean and sharpen garden tools

Service the lawn mower and/or pool filter equipment

Check outside for minor repairs—walls, fence, gates, roof, windows, paint work, rust patches

Clean all garden furniture and rustproof if necessary

Although these jobs come under the 'spring cleaning' heading, your annual routine can be at the beginning of autumn or at the start of summer. Pick a time when your energy is up and there are lots of hands around to help. It is often a good time to think about having a garage sale—you might clear out things that someone else would treasure. It is also the time to make dates with professional tradespeople to do the jobs you physically cannot do yourself or for which you don't have the right equipment.

CLEANING EQUIPMENT

The cleaning tool you choose for each job—whether it's the vacuum cleaner or an old cotton sock—can be the key to successful cleaning. The surfaces and materials in your home will determine what cleaning equipment you need to have on hand. If you employ a cleaner and they bring all their own equipment, maybe you will only need the basic broom, mop, bucket and dusting cloth for emergencies.

Recycled clothing and household items make excellent cleaning cloths and equipment. The towel that has finally gone into holes can be used as a general mop-up cloth. Old cotton socks are great for covering the broom head to clean off cobwebs. Toothbrushes are marvellous for those hard-to-get-at corners and wonderful for gently polishing jewellery. Well-worn and well-loved t-shirts can be great for polishing the floors and if you forget to recycle the odd newspaper use it to give a good shine when cleaning the windows.

SOME SPECIALISED EQUIPMENT

There are many types of specialised cleaning equipment available. Their considerable price tags mean you'd need to be a fairly serious cleaner to warrant the purchase. If you do a lot of cleaning or have a large house and/or family, though, they may be worth considering. A few are listed below.

Microfibre cleaning cloths assist in dusting and general cleaning. Their tiny synthetic fibres split in different ways to trap dust and dirt. The overall efficiency of these types of cloths is remarkable, and they can mean you save on water and detergents. Like all useful cleaning tools, proper maintenance and care of them will give a longer life span

BASIC EQUIPMENT

2 buckets

mop bucket

sponge mop

cotton mop

floor-dusting mop

long-handled soft broom

yard or stiff broom

small brush and pan

stiff scrubbing brush

soft scrubbing brush

bottle-cleaning brush

toothbrush

toilet brush (for each toilet)

feather duster

dusting cloths

vacuum cleaner

steel wool

large sponge

spray bottles

rubber gloves

cotton gloves

cleaning apron

lint-free cloth

to their cleaning efficiency. They need to be washed regularly in warm soapy water to remove collected dust and dirt.

Electric steam cleaners sanitise surfaces by producing a continuous shot of steam by heating water to a high temperature, working a bit like a steam iron. These cleaners can be used on hard surface floors, although are not recommended for cork tiles. They can also be used on rugs and carpets, mattresses and some upholstery.

Outdoor water blasters are designed to clean concrete driveways and sandstone paving. These electric outdoor appliances are excellent for removing mould and dirt. Some may have attachments that can be used to clean roof tiles and guttering, as well as a brush for cleaning cars. It is useful if outside areas attract mould due to damp causing the surface to become very slippery. To remove grease stains and other oily stains try kerosene first, then use the water blaster with mild detergent.

Storing and maintaining equipment

Try to hang mops and brooms up off the floor in a cupboard or laundry area. Keep cloths, sponges and smaller cleaning items in a storage container that can be wheeled out or carried around. A small shopping trolley, a basket with a handle, a bucket or a child's toy wagon are ideal for this task. If you have upstairs and downstairs areas to clean, think about having two sets to save carrying everything up and down.

Household cleaning products and other chemicals must be stored out of the reach of

---

THE BASIC CLEANERS YOU WILL NEED ARE:

dishwashing liquid

general-purpose mild household cleaner

abrasive household cleaner

furniture polish

metal cleaners (brass, silver, stainless steel)

floor polish

laundry detergents and aids (woolwash, biological or enzyme detergent, bleach, fabric softener)

disinfectant

Other useful products include household ammonia, white vinegar, borax, methylated spirits, mineral turpentine, linseed oil, turpentine, talcum powder, eucalyptus oil, bicarbonate of soda, glycerine and vaseline.

children and pets. Ideally they should be locked in a cupboard safe from spills and inquisitive little hands and tongues.

Maintain your cleaning equipment regularly. Always rinse and dry mops and floor sponges thoroughly after use. Brooms and small brushes should be washed in mild detergent and then rinsed and hung up to dry, at least every couple of months. Wipe over the vacuum cleaner with a warm damp cloth to remove dust and dirt, and make sure the bag is replaced regularly (some vacuum cleaners have a light which goes on when the bag is full in case you forget to check). Filters in vacuum cleaners should also be changed regularly. Check the power cord for wear and tear. Dusters and cleaning cloths should be washed regularly but if they are ingrained with dirt, throw them out. If you are recycling towels, T-shirts and other materials you may never have to buy new cloths and you'll save on cleaning expenses.

There are as many types of electric floor cleaners as there are floor coverings. The most important is, of course, the vacuum cleaner. Floor polishers and carpet shampoo machines are easily hired, which is more economical than having them in the cleaning cupboard to use only once a year. The types of vacuum cleaners available, which each have their good and bad points, include upright, cylinder, water/dry, miniature and hand-held cordless vacuum cleaners.

CLEANING PRODUCTS

There are many cleaning products on the market for every type of cleaning job. Our ancestors had simple recipes for cleaners and they probably cooked them up on the stove alongside the soup stock. We can continue the trend and brew up our own (see chapter 9) or use commercial products recommended for the job. Many cleaners contain hazardous chemicals and these must be stored out of the reach of children and pets. (For information about household cleaning products see chapter 8.) Never mix different cleaners as this could create a dangerous chemical reaction. Always wear protective gloves and clothing if using caustic products and make sure the area or room is well ventilated. Most product labels should list instructions for use and warnings: make sure you always study the labels before using a new product and follow the manufacturer's advice. See the list at left for basic cleaning products.

HIRING CLEANING HELP

It is important to be honest with yourself when it comes to household cleaning. If you prefer to do other things than drag the vacuum cleaner around, then budgeting for professional cleaning help should be considered as a household expense. Who hasn't heard someone moaning that they cannot keep on top of their household chores but would feel guilty about paying someone to do it for them? Many people who hire a cleaner spend hours cleaning the house before the cleaner comes as they feel guilty about the out-of-control mess that has accumulated and they do not want the paid cleaner to see it! Put the guilt feelings aside.

If you decide that regular help is needed, the next step is to list the things you want done and how often. If you want someone to do everything from the cleaning to washing, ironing and putting away then a housekeeper could be the person for you. If you need a cleaner, cook, nanny, chauffeur and odd-job person you might need live-in staff—but make sure you have the space and the bank balance. Realistically defining the jobs you want done is essential for briefing a prospective helper and working out how many hours you need them for and how often. If your budget is small, perhaps a few hours once a fortnight to tackle the hard jobs may be what you need.

Cost

After you've worked out what you need, estimate how long you take to clean your house and use this as a guide when quoted an hourly rate. Ask friends what they pay for a cleaning service and how many hours it covers, with how many people working and how frequent the service is. Get several quotes from professional cleaning companies and domestic help agencies and do a comparison. The most expensive quote might not be the best.

Another thing to consider is the standard of cleaning you want. Find out what your prospective cleaner does for their other clients and work out how high or low the standard is. Some freelance cleaners will bring all their own equipment and others will expect you to provide it. If you are going to provide all the cleaning equipment and products, this has to be a factor in the cost.

Where to look for good help

Having made the decision to hire someone to help keep the dust at bay, the next thing to do is ask friends and neighbours if they can recommend a reliable service. Alternatively, try the local papers, the *Yellow Pages* and community noticeboards. The prerequisites when considering hiring a cleaner are reliability, honesty and consistency. If you are going to be out while the cleaner is in your home it is important to feel comfortable and to trust that the work will be carried out and that your home is secure. Obtain at least four references —and make sure they are not relatives or friends—and make a phone check of each one. Find out the length of employment, reliability and standard of work. If you have any doubts try another service.

Another way to find a cleaner is to seek the services of a reliable domestic employment agency. Agencies screen all their cleaning personnel and will try to send the same person each time you require the service. If the cleaner is sick they will send someone in their place. They charge a placement fee which is collected by the cleaner when you pay them. Normally they expect to be there for four hours to do a thorough job and to be paid an hourly rate. The cleaners will expect you to provide all the cleaning equipment and products.

You can also have your home regularly cleaned by a professional cleaning company. They will come to your home and give you a quote for the job. They should provide the same person each visit, guarantee their work and provide all the cleaning equipment and products needed for the job.

As well as checking references it's important to find out what insurance cover the cleaner has. Some cleaners will have their own personal accident and liability cover. Your own household insurance policy may cover your liability as an employer of a domestic person. Check with your insurance company and if you are not covered, find out if it can be added to your household insurance and what the extra cost will be. If using an agency, check that anyone they send is covered for personal accident and liability. It is important to have the matter of insurance sorted out before the cleaner starts.

Once you have agreed on a price for the cleaning find out the preferred method of payment. It may be easier to pay by cheque or cash, or pay monthly on receipt of an invoice. Work out what is best for you and the cleaner.

How to brief your cleaner

When interviewing a prospective cleaner make sure you show them all through your home. Give them a list of jobs and explain the routine you would like carried out. Go through it carefully and make sure they understand. If you want certain chores carried out once a month put this on the list, too. Establish what cleaning equipment and products they will bring or what you will provide. Any cleaner worth their polish will have general knowledge about cleaning different surfaces and objects. If you are not sure, ask them what they will use or tell them what you like the surfaces to be cleaned with. Some cleaners will not want to clean antique china or glass, or polish your silver, so check this out at the interview. Maybe your joy will be to sit down once a month and clean the family heirlooms while the cleaner does the oven.

Once you have made a decision about who you will hire to clean your home, introduce them to all the household members and any pets. It is always a good idea to have a trial period of say a month to establish a pattern and standard. This gives you both the option to review the service after the trial period.

If you are not going to be at home when they call, you'll need to supply spare keys. If you have a burglar alarm system instruct them how turn it off (and set it when they leave), or if you do not feel secure about them doing this at first, switch it off while they are there. If you live in a security building, let the neighbours know that you have a cleaner calling regularly in case they worry about a stranger going in and out of your apartment while you are out.

Establishing a trusting relationship with your cleaner is very important. Remember you are employing someone to make your life easier: if you find the standard of cleaning drops or the cleaners are there for shorter hours than agreed, bring it to their attention. As with any repetitive job a little bit of variety in the routine will make it more interesting, so include a variety of jobs to be carried out seasonally. Finally if you treat your employee well and offer a word of praise for a job well done, a bonus or gift at holiday time, you will help create a mutual appreciation and respect and a successful long-term relationship.

Specialist cleaning services

Some cleaning jobs are beyond the pail of the most diligent cleaner and a specialist has to be called in. Again, word of mouth can really be the best source of information which guarantees the workmanship. Also, when purchasing new household goods like a rug or curtains, ask the manufacturer or supplier for instructions about cleaning. Keep handy a file of 'Household Information' with warranty or product instructions or other information in it, to refer to when you need it. (When you come to sell your home this information is useful for the next owner if they are purchasing the fixtures and fittings.)

Any service you may think of hiring should be able to supply you with references you can check. A few phone calls may save you the cost of replacing carpets or curtains after a poor cleaning job. Special offers from specialist cleaning companies sometimes pop up in the letter box— check them out before taking them up on their money-saving offer.

You can also hire cleaning equipment and do it yourself, which is another way of making sure you get the job done properly. All cleaning units should come with simple, easy-to-follow instructions. Check first that you are using the right equipment for the job—do not steam clean the wallpaper unless you want it to come off! Rental companies are listed in the phone book or local papers and charge a daily or weekly hire fee; some supermarkets also rent carpet-cleaning equipment.

You can find a professional service to clean just about everything. The experts should be called in if you have an oil painting that needs cleaning and restoring or an antique wedding gown to be specially cleaned. Although I cover lots of household items and products in this book, don't try cleaning anything precious or valuable unless you really know what you're doing. Take such items to a specialist with the proper knowledge and training.

HOUSEHOLD RUBBISH AND RECYCLING

When it comes to household rubbish, there are ways to reuse many of the things that get thrown away. Here are just some ideas.

Recycling

CLOTHING

- Swap clothes amongst friends, especially children's clothes, or take them down to the local registered charity.
- Cut up t-shirts and other soft clothing and use as cloths in the kitchen or for polishing shoes and silver.

- Patchwork cushions or bedcovers can be made from discarded clothes—make an heirloom piece to be handed down.
- Trousers make good shorts or a clothes-peg bag—cut off the legs and stitch along the bottom.
- Tights or stockings are terrific for securing plants to stakes. They're also great for getting flies off windscreens and any cleaning job that requires a scourer.
- Shirts come in handy as clothing protection when painting or to cover a fur coat. Cut off the buttons if making into cleaning rags.
- Dress-up box—commit the most outrageous worst buys! There will always be an occasion for fancy dress or fun children's dress up games.

PAPER
- Line drawers with old wrapping paper.
- Make gift tags out of old greetings cards.
- Use in craft projects like collage or papier mâché.
- Stuff into shoes or boots to help keep their shape.
- Shred newspaper for disease-free animal bedding.
- Clean windows with scrunched-up newspaper.
- Paper bags—ripen fruit in a paper bag; sweat capsicum once they have been chargrilled in paper bags to help remove the skins; decorate plain ones to make interesting wrapping paper.
- Egg cartons—use as seedling sprouters or to store sewing pieces like buttons, beads, sequins.
- Old magazines—swap with friends, take to old people's home, medical centre or sell to collectors if you have some really old ones.
- Envelopes—staple together and make phone notepads.

PLASTIC BOTTLES AND JARS
- Plastic bottles with handles—cut the bottoms off and use as a loudhailer at sporting games when coaching or just watching!
- Shampoo bottles and the likes—fill with water and freeze to use as ice bricks for eskies.
- Use ice-cream containers to freeze sauces or food items. Yoghurt cartons and takeaway food containers are great for storing food or stationery items such as rubberbands and paperclips.
- Store water in drink bottles in the fridge during summer.
- Plastic containers with lids can be used to store screws and other hardware bits and pieces.
- Round butter or margarine containers can be used for saucers for indoor plants.

GLASS JARS AND BOTTLES

- Store nails, wallplugs, hooks, all sorts of handyman bits and pieces.
- Use for homemade jams and sauces, cordials and pickles.
- Store salad dressings and marinades in the refrigerator.
- Fill a wine bottle with icy cold water, cork firmly and use to roll-out pastry.

PLASTIC BAGS

These are one of the world's greatest pollutants. They cause great devastation to our wild life, especially in our oceans.

Firstly try and say *no* to plastic bags and take your own shopping bag or trolley, keep reusing the same ones every time you shop. Leave them in the car or shopping basket. Keep plastic bags that do make their way into your home in a storage bag.

These can be then be used to:

- line wastebins
- tie bundles of newspapers or magazines together
- use as a freezer bag—label on the outside what it is
- cover a cake or other baked items to prevent them from drying out in the fridge
- use as a cape when doing a home hair-tinting session. Place another bag over your hair while you wait for the tint to take.
- use as a glove to grease a cake tin or tray
- keep one near the phone if you are having a messy cooking day—a plastic bag over your hand saves you covering the phone with goo should it ring!
- place seasoned flour in a bag and use to toss food for a dish that re-quires coating lightly with flour
- wrap shoes and other items in plastic bags when packing for holidays. Take extra plastic bags to use as dirty-laundry bags.
- carry toiletries in plastic bags when travelling
- store herbs and lettuce leaves in the fridge
- place a wet paint brush in a plastic bag if you need a break from painting as it will prevent the paint from drying out.

SOME EXTRA THINGS TO RECYCLE

- Use an old teapot as a string holder— the string can be pulled out the spout! Or use to plant bulbs or as a simple vase for herbs and flowers.
- Place spare keys on a shower curtain ring.
- Keep clothes pegs in a mesh orange bag, or store children's bath toys in it.

- An old shaving brush is great for polishing shoes or metal.
- Milk cartons can make great firelighters.
- Refill an empty roll-on deodorant bottle with sunscreen for roll-on sun protection.
- Fill hot water bottles with air or warm water and rest your neck while soaking in a hot bath.

Chapter 2

CLEANING THE HOUSE

THE KITCHEN

We all spend a lot of time in the kitchen and it is probably one of the easiest places to keep clean. As you wait for the kettle to boil, the cupboard fronts could have a quick wipe and the teapot could be given a lovely shine. But it can also get really out of hand, especially when you're preparing a large feast, and after it! Everyone seems to leave piles of clutter like bills, newspapers, magazines and letters on the kitchen table or benchtops. Cupboards get overcrowded and spills and drips occur. The fridge and freezer get congested with almost empty jars and unlabelled leftovers which are often way past their use-by date.

In the kitchen, hygiene and the control of bacteria are essential and are an important factor in our choice of cleaning products. Any surface where food is to be prepared has to be cleaned during and after use, and equipment and utensils must be cleaned thoroughly before being stored.

If you are lucky enough to plan your own kitchen layout from scratch, make sure the storage systems and power sockets as well as appliances are all conveniently placed so that it is an easy and harmonious area to work in. If you inherit someone else's kitchen design and you find yourself walking all over the place to get the things you need most often, think about replacing the cupboards. It can take several months to design a really good workable system in the kitchen but the time invested will make it an easier and a more efficient place to work in and keep clean.

Kitchen fittings and equipment

BENCHTOPS AND WORK SURFACES

Benchtops can be made from laminate, Corian, stainless steel, wood, tiles, slate, granite and marble and should always be cleaned after food preparation.

Corian Clean as for laminated surfaces, but you can use a gentle scourer for stubborn stains and marks. Matt, semi-gloss and high-gloss finishes should be treated in order of finish—heavy scouring for matt and lighter for the other two finishes. Difficult stains and marks can be removed with very fine sandpaper and then polished and cleaned off with a soft cloth.

Engineered stone or rock, sometimes known as querella stone or Caesar stone, is made from crushed marble, quartz and resin. It is a sealed surface, and therefore not porous like marble or granite. To keep clean wipe over with a hot with damp cloth. Clean stubborn greasy stains or marks with a few drops of 1% cloudy ammonia diluted in water (see Floors page 28 and Bathrooms page 33).

Granite An attractive natural surface which is polished stone; it is not sealed and is therefore quite porous. To clean, wipe over regularly with a hot damp cloth. Use a few drops of household ammonia in water to clean up greasy stains or marks.

Laminate Do not scratch the top by cutting food on it and never use a scourer to remove stains. It will stand heat up to 250–300 °C from hot pans and other cooking utensils, but it can be damaged if they are left standing for a long period. Clean with hot water and detergent and use a few drops of eucalyptus oil in the water as a disinfectant. To remove stains, rub with neat detergent or white vinegar, leave for a few minutes and then rinse. Window cleaner can be used for a smear-free finish.

Marble More porous than granite, so care must be taken not to slosh water around which will soak into it. Wipe over with a hot damp cloth which has been dipped in water and a mild detergent.

Slate Clean with hot water and a mild detergent only. Wipe over with a little lemon oil to give the slate a lovely shine and polish off with a soft dry cloth.

Stainless steel *see* Sinks, stainless steel (page 17)

Tiles Glazed ceramic tiled benchtops should be washed with hot water and detergent. Bad stains or marks can be removed by rubbing a little salt over the spot with a cut lemon. Clean the grout with a toothbrush dipped in a solution of ammonia and water, rinse off and wipe over with a clean damp cloth.

Wood, sealed   Wipe over with warm water and remember not to use it as a chopping board. Do not place anything hot on this surface—put hot pots and pans on a tile or wooden chopping board. Bad burn marks will need to be sanded back and resealed.

Wood, unsealed   Rub over with boiled linseed oil (several applications may be necessary) and wipe off excess with a soft cloth. Wipe over regularly with oil as for wooden chopping boards to prevent cracking and drying out. Use a little salt and cut lemon on stains or scorch marks.

SINKS

Sinks are usually made from stainless steel, enamel, Corian and sometimes acrylic.

Acrylic   Clean with hot water and detergent and remove stains with white vinegar. Never use scourers or abrasive cleaners; any small scratches can be removed with metal polish.

Corian   Usually a matt finish and easy to keep clean with a gentle scourer and detergent. To clean the sink, fill with 1 part household bleach to 4 parts water. Leave for 30 minutes, then rinse away and dry.

Enamel   Use hot water and detergent to clean—bleach or abrasive scourers will damage, scratch and yellow the sink. Treat stains by rubbing a little powdered borax over the spot with a cut lemon. For stubborn stains make a paste with bicarbonate of soda and hydrogen peroxide and rub it over the area; wear gloves and have the area well ventilated. Let the paste dry, then thoroughly rinse it off.

Stainless steel   Clean with hot water and detergent and dry with a soft cloth. Never use any abrasive cleaners or scourers. Stains can be removed by rubbing neat detergent over the spot. Polish the dry sink with a soft cloth and methylated spirits.

SINK DRAIN

Sinks should have a removable drainer to catch any food debris, keeping the drain free from anything that might block it. Never pour tea leaves, milk or cream, coffee grains, oil or grease down the sink. To keep your drains smelling sweet, fill a jug with a mixture of 2 tablespoons bicarbonate of soda in 750 mL white vinegar and pour it down the sink. Leave overnight or for at least 30 minutes, then clear by running very hot water down the drain.

SINK WASTE DISPOSAL UNIT

As with ordinary sinks do not put tea leaves, coffee grains, milk, oil or grease into it and follow the manufacturer's instruction about what is safe to dispose of through the unit. To keep it smelling sweet, cut up a lemon or an orange and put through the disposal unit with 1–2 cups of white vinegar; be careful not to let cutlery, cloths and other small items jam it up.

TAPS

A toothbrush will remove any built up dirt round the base of the tap or any other area hard to reach with a cloth; use hot water and detergent. ***Brass and copper*** If they have a lacquered finish, wipe clean with damp wet cloth. Otherwise use a proprietary polish. If there are tarnish or verdigris marks, make a paste with salt and lemon juice and rub gently until the marks come off. If really stubborn, wipe over with household ammonia, rinse and dry off with a soft cloth and then polish. ***Chrome*** Clean and polish with a cloth soaked in white vinegar or a few drops of water and ammonia. Use a toothbrush to get into difficult crevices. ***Gold plated*** Wash with warm water and detergent and buff dry with a soft cloth. If tarnish marks occur, wipe off with household ammonia, then rinse and buff dry. ***Stainless steel*** Clean with hot water and detergent, and wipe dry. Polish when dry with methylated spirits.

GARBAGE BINS

Try to have three bins to collect kitchen rubbish—one for clean paper and bottles for recycling, one for food scraps to be composted and one for general rubbish. Empty the compost and general rubbish bins daily to stop unpleasant odours and for hygiene. If you cannot compost, place all food scraps in the general bin. Line the bins with a plastic bin liner—plastic shopping bags will sometimes fit, depending on the size of the bin. Wipe out the empty bins with ammonia and warm water and if stained give them a gentle scrub with a plastic scourer. Rub a little tea-tree oil or eucalyptus oil round the top to keep them smelling fresh.

COOKTOPS

After use always wipe clean with hot water and detergent to prevent a build-up of grease and food stains. The materials most commonly used for cooktops are vitreous enamel and stainless steel and to avoid damage or scratching never use gritty cleaners. Vinegar, milk, citrus and other acid foods can stain if the spills are not wiped up immediately.

Ceramic   Wipe over with a damp cloth to remove any spillage or drips. Sugary sauces may be harder to remove so use a plastic scourer and warm soapy water to remove any stubborn marks. Dry with a soft clean cloth. If the base of cookware is dirty it may damage the cooktop, so make sure cookware is clean before using.

Electric   Make sure the cooktop is turned off before you start cleaning. Take apart any bits that can be soaked in the sink or put in the dishwasher. Never soak any electrical parts in water.

Gas   Most cooktops will come apart for cleaning and can be soaked in hot water and detergent to loosen cooked-on stains. Use a plastic scouring pad to help remove any built-up food deposits. Some parts may be washed in the dishwasher after loosening any hard food stains by soaking. If it is really dirty use a caustic cleaner and a toothbrush to get into difficult areas. Leave on for a couple of hours and then scrub off with hot water.

Induction   Only cookware with a magnetic base such as stainless steel, enamelled cast iron and steel pots and pans should be used on induction cooktops. If any spillage occurs, wipe over with a damp cloth and dry with a soft dry cloth. This type of cooktop is an energy-efficient method of cooking.

Solid fuel   These hotplates will normally burn off any food deposits. To clean, wipe over with a gentle scouring liquid and then rinse off with a hot damp cloth. Use a stiff wire brush on the hotplates to remove any crumbs or food build-up. Wipe over occasionally with a little vegetable oil to prevent rust.

GRILL PANS

As with other baking pans always wash after use in hot water and detergent. Allowing grease to build up in the grill pan can cause a fire hazard. Scrape out any solid fat or grease with a flexible kitchen spatula. Soak in hot water and detergent to help remove any difficult baked-on grease and use a plastic scourer.

OVERHEAD EXTRACTOR FANS

Wipe over with a hot damp cloth to remove any grease or moisture after each use. Regularly replace the filter and take the appliance apart to clean with hot water and detergent.

OVENS

The main problem with oven cleaners (and why most people don't like to use them and therefore put off cleaning the oven) is the strong fumes from caustic soda and solvents in most products. An alternative is to clean regularly with less caustic products like washing soda, which is a mild alkali. This product comes in crystal or powder form and should be diluted with water (¼ cup to 2 litres of water). Wipe over the oven and use a nylon scourer for stubborn stains or spills that have become caked on.

Each type of oven should have specific manufacturer's cleaning instructions. Most ovens are enamel and not self-cleaning. Wipe out the oven every time you use it with a hot damp cloth and always clean up any spills on the oven floor to prevent a build-up of cooked-on food. To loosen grease, place half a cup of cloudy ammonia into a warm oven, turn the oven off and close the door. Leave for several hours or overnight. Wipe out with hot water and detergent. For stubborn spills use a commercial oven cleaner and a nylon scourer.

The most successful way to clean an oven is to clean up spills as they happen. Wait for the oven to cool down before using kitchen towel or newspaper to mop up. Wipe the oven over with kitchen towel or damp cloth as it cools down.

When cooking a roast, use an oven bag to prevent splattering over the interior of the oven.

Glass splashback   Wipe over with damp cloth and clean any greasy marks with a wet sponge and detergent. Dry with a clean lint-free cloth.

Oven doors   Most oven doors are glass and enamel or stainless steel with a rubber seal. Clean with hot water and detergent. Some oven doors can be removed for easier cleaning.

Oven shelves and supports   Most of these parts are removable and should be washed in hot water and detergent. If very soiled soak in a mixture of 1 part washing soda mixed with 4 parts hot water (use the bath or laundry tub if they will not fit in the sink).

Oven with steam function These have the added bonus of self-cleaning by creating steam within the oven to loosen any grease or spillage. Use this function at the end of cooking as the oven cools down. The oven can be wiped over when cool with a cloth or kitchen paper.

Pyrolytic ovens are promoted as the 'true self-cleaning oven'. A safety lock in the door seals the oven, then the oven is heated to a very high temperature (around 500 °C) and stubborn residues are burn off. Any food spillage is reduced to ash that can then be wiped or brushed out of the oven. Follow the manufacturer's instructions for use and cleaning.

Self-cleaning ovens   These ovens save a lot of elbow grease. They are coated with a catalytic enamel lining and the manufacturer's instructions will tell you how to care for it. Never use any scourer or oven cleaner on these surfaces. Generally the walls and floor of the oven only need wiping over with a hot damp cloth and any burnt ashes can be swept out with a soft brush. Any removable parts can be washed in hot soapy water.

MICROWAVE OVENS

Wipe the inside walls and floor with a hot damp cloth to remove any cooking stains. Take out any removable parts and wash in hot water and detergent. For stubborn stains place a bowl of hot water in the oven and cook on high for about six minutes. Allow to stand for a few minutes and then remove. Wipe the inside over with a soft cloth. Always wipe up spills immediately. Clean the door and the outside of the oven with a hot damp cloth and detergent. It is important to use the right size of cooking dish to prevent spills in the first place. Follow manufacturer's instructions for size of cooking dishes, power strength and cooking time.

DISHWASHERS

Use a recommended dishwasher detergent and never use too much as this will dull the stainless steel inside the machine. To clean a dull interior, run the machine empty through a short wash cycle with two cups of vinegar.

WASHING WITH A DISHWASHER

Scrape food debris from plates and other items as when washing up by hand, and rinse.

Soak items as necessary to loosen cooked-on food.

Always load the dishwasher to its full capacity before running it. It is uneconomical to run a half-empty machine.

Rinse dishes as they are used and fill the machine up during the day.

Make sure the filters are clean and that any tall items will not obstruct the water jets.

Do not place stainless steel and silver items in the same basket or touching each other in the tray (can cause pitting to the silver).

Only wash items which are recommended for the dishwasher. Delicate, heat-sensitive or wooden items, glass or china with metal trim, cut glass, lacquered items, antique china or glasses are the most likely to be damaged or break in the dishwasher.

Read the manufacturer's instructions about what is safe to put in the dishwasher and how to obtain the most efficient use of your machine.

Clean the cabinet and around the door seal of the machine with hot water and detergent and use a soft brush if built-up dirt is difficult to remove. Clean filters regularly (check manufacturer's instructions) and check for broken glass, stray cutlery or jar labels in the bottom of the dishwasher. Dishwasher detergent is very caustic so keep out reach of children and pets.

REFRIGERATORS

To clean the inside wipe over with a hot damp cloth dipped in a solution of 1 part bicarbonate of soda to 7 parts of water. Finish off by wiping over the inside walls and floor with a clean damp cloth and a little vanilla essence. Any removable parts can be washed in hot water and detergent. To clean the door seals and prevent mould forming, wipe over with a little methylated spirits or white vinegar. After cleaning, the cabinet can be polished with car polish. To clean the refrigerator coils at the back of the fridge, turn the power off and use a soft brush or vacuum cleaner with a soft brush attachment to remove dust or dirt. If you empty your fridge and leave it turned off for any period of time, leave the door open and wipe the inside with vinegar to prevent mould forming.

Alutec This is a brushed aluminium finish which does not show finger-marks as with other metal finished fridges or ovens. Grease or other food marks or stains can be removed with a warm cloth and a gentle plastic scourer.

Wipe over with a dry cloth after cleaning.

Stainless steel has grown in popularity as a finish in kitchens as well as laundries and bathrooms (fridge, stove tops, dishwashers). There are many appliances in the kitchen which have a stainless steel finish, and cleaning them can present a challenge. Water will leave marks when it dries, so dry any wet areas with a soft dry cloth. Wipe over any marks with a damp cloth using hot water and detergent. Polish dry with a soft cloth. Very stubborn marks can be removed using a plastic scourer and stainless steel cream cleanser, then polish dry with a soft cloth. Methylated spirits will remove greasy marks. Regardless of which method is used for cleaning, it is imperative to polish dry with a soft dry cloth.

FREEZERS

Defrost according to manufacturer's instructions at least twice a year or when the freezer is nearly empty. Wash any removable parts in hot water and detergent and wipe the inside of the defrosted cabinet with 1 part bicarbonate of soda mixed with 7 parts warm water. As with fridges, if you leave the freezer switched off and empty for any period, leave the door open and wipe the inside over with vinegar to stop mould forming.

SMALL ELECTRICAL APPLIANCES

Those invaluable electrical gadgets that we can't live without—electric can opener, food processor, blender, spice grinder, carving knife, coffee grinder, knife sharpener, whisk, fry pan, char-grill pan, bread maker, scales, toaster, griller, wok, steamer, citrus juicer, and so on. Always turn off the power and remove the plug from the power point and the other end from the appliance if it's not fixed. Consult the manufacturer's instructions on cleaning. Take the gadget apart where applicable and clean each part separately. Never immerse electrical parts in water unless otherwise specified by the manufacturer.

Do not immerse sharp blades, slicing discs or knives in the sink. Rinse well first and clean under hot running water using a soft brush to remove any food. Carefully dry and store. Always wipe the appliance with a warm damp cloth after each use to remove any grease or food and use a small brush or baby-bottle cleaning brush to get at difficult areas.

Crumbs from the toaster can be shaken out of the bottom and a small brush used gently to remove any debris collected inside.

Any chrome appliance can be cleaned by wiping over with a mixture of bicarbonate of soda and a few drops of water. Can opener teeth can be cleaned with a toothbrush and warm soapy water. Rub a little cooking oil over the teeth after cleaning.

Food processor bowls and other plastic removable parts may be washed in the dishwasher but remember dishwasher detergent and heat can cause the plastic to become brittle and discolour and the life of the part may be diminished.

Electric juice extractor Take the extractor apart after use, remove all the food debris and clean every part while it is still wet from the juicing. These appliances usually come apart and can be washed in warm soapy water. The very fine sieve should be cleaned with a plastic scourer and hard-bristle washing up brush. Rinse under cold running water. If the machine is not cleaned straight away, it may be necessary to soak the parts to loosen any food debris. Always follow the manufacturer's instructions on maintenance and cleaning.

CHOPPING BOARDS

Plastic   Scrub with a small brush with hot water and detergent or wash in the dishwasher. Chopping boards can be wiped over with a very mild solution of household bleach (a few drops to a litre of water) to kill any surface bacteria. Remember for hygiene to use different boards for different foods—mark the corner so that they can be easily identified. Raw and cooked meats should be prepared on different boards, and chilli especially should have a board of its own.

Wood   Season the wood by rubbing with a little vegetable oil to protect them from splitting or warping. Scrub them well with a stiff brush and hot water to remove any food or stains. Food smells can be removed by rubbing some salt with the cut side of half a lemon over the board. Rinse off and drain. Store in an airy dry place on their long edge.

POTS AND PANS

Made from a variety of materials and need different treatment when cleaning.

Aluminium   Clean in hot water and detergent, using a scourer if necessary. For bad stains and discolouration boil up 2 teaspoonfuls of cream of tartar with 1 litre of water. Alternatively, apple peelings or citrus peelings may be boiled up with some water in the pan.

Burnt frypans or saucepans Place the base of a very hot burnt pan into a sink filled with warm water to stop the cooking from the base. Soak burnt hot pans with hot water first, as this will help the cooked-on food to loosen as the water cools down. Then wash the inside of the pan with hot water.

Never use washing soda or dishwasher detergent to soak or clean aluminium saucepans as it will discolour and damage the metal interior. Use a plastic scourer to remove stuck-on food, steel wool may harm the surface.

Enamelled cast-iron pans should be soaked with hot water to remove burnt-on food. Use a plastic scourer and detergent to remove any debris that may still remain after soaking.

Cast iron   Season new cookware with oil. This is easy to do—brush the pot, pan or saucepan with flavour-free vegetable oil and pour in enough to cover the bottom. Gently heat over a low flame or in the oven for at least an hour. Remove from the heat and allow to cool. Pour out the oil (keep for frying) and wipe out with a kitchen paper towel.

After using the cookware, wash with hot water and detergent then thoroughly dry. Brush a little oil into the pan before storing.

Copper   Never scour as it will damage the lining. Wash in hot water and detergent. To remove any stuck-on food, fill the pan with warm water and allow to soak. Make sure copper is cleaned thoroughly as green-rust stains are poisonous. Polish the outside with a combination of vinegar and salt, then rinse and polish dry. If preferred, used a commercial copper cleaner, always following the instructions.

Earthenware, glazed   Wash in hot water and detergent. Use a plastic scourer to remove difficult food stains after soaking in hot water.

Earthenware, unglazed   Before using, season the cookware by soaking it in water; this stops food juices being absorbed into the pottery. Wash in hot water but never use detergent. Soak in hot water if the food is difficult to remove. Never scour unglazed surfaces.

Enamel   A coating on aluminium, cast-iron or pressed steel pans and baking dishes. Season first as with cast-iron cookware. Wash with hot water and detergent and use a gentle plastic scouring pad to help remove stubborn food stains. Handle carefully to avoid chipping the enamel.

Glass   Wash in hot water and detergent and use a plastic scourer if necessary to remove burnt-on food. Can be washed in the dishwasher.

Non-stick materials   Never use scourers, just wash in hot water and detergent. If burnt-on food is hard to remove, soak in warm water.

Plastic   Used for cookware handles, microwave cookware, measuring jugs, kitchen utensils and mixing bowls. Wash in hot water and detergent, and be careful not to scratch plastic as the marks may become stained and can harbour bacteria. Will melt at high temperatures so not suitable to be washed in dishwashers.

Stainless steel   Clean in hot water and detergent. You can use a scourer if you are not worried about removing the initial shine. Can be washed in the dishwasher, but first scrape out any food debris.

Tinware   Many baking trays, patty tins, cake tins, and so on are still made of tin, which can be seasoned as with cast iron to prevent rusting. Avoid the use of a scourer and wash in hot water and detergent. Some baking ware manufacturers suggest using hot water but no detergent. Refer to care instructions when purchasing new tinware. Always thoroughly dry after washing by placing in a cooling oven.

TABLEWARE

Whether you eat off china, porcelain, glazed or unglazed earthenware, glass or enamel, it should all be handled carefully if you want it to last.

Bone china and porcelain   The most delicate tableware which needs careful attention. Extremes of heat and abrasive detergents are the most common cause of damage and breakages. Check manufacturer's instructions to see if it is safe to wash in a dishwasher. If there is metallic glaze pattern or hand-painted design, never use an abrasive cleaner or wash in the dishwasher. If it is very fine or old china it should be washed by hand. Scrape off excess food scraps with a rubber or plastic spatula and rinse promptly as certain acidic foods can stain. To protect it from chipping while washing use a plastic bowl or place an old towel in the bottom of the sink. Use a mild detergent and warm water. Rinse off with warm water and dry.

Earthenware or stoneware, glazed or unglazed, see Pots and pans (page 24)

Enamel see Pots and pans (page 24)

Everyday china   The dinner service that gets used the most and probably treated the roughest should be washed as for bone china and porcelain. If it was very inexpensive, it can be prone to chipping, the glaze may craze and a pattern may fade if continually washed in the dishwasher.

Glass see Pots and pans (page 24)

CUTLERY

Some cutlery will need special care when cleaning. If purchasing new cutlery, check the manufacturer's instructions. Sterling silver or silver plate and stainless steel are the most common metals used for cutlery.

Cutlery with handles of bone, ivory, wood or porcelain should never be immersed in water. Soak the metal parts only in warm water and detergent, gently use a soft brush to remove food, rinse in hot water and dry immediately. The handles should be wiped over with a hot damp cloth and then dried.

Sharp cook's knives should never be immersed in water for safety reasons but also because the handles could warp in hot water, or if washed in the dishwasher, and subsequently warp the knife. To remove stains use a little salt sprinkled on half a lemon and rub along the blade. For any difficult stains on carbon steel knives use a scouring pad or a wet cork dipped in scouring powder, but be careful not to blunt the edge.

Bronze   Thai bronze cutlery should be washed as for stainless steel. Polish when dry with a soft cloth. If it has wooden handles, wash by hand. Remove any green spots or stains by rubbing the area with a soft cloth dipped in pure turpentine, then rinse thoroughly and wipe dry.

Stainless steel   Wash in hot water and detergent or in the dishwasher but do not use steel wool to clean off stains. Polish when dry with a soft cloth. Acidic or salty foods can cause pit marks so always rinse cutlery immediately after use. Polish with a proprietary stainless steel polish if necessary.

Sterling silver or silver plate   If it is in use every day and is not antique, wash in hot water and detergent, rinse in hot water and dry immediately. A proprietary cleaner can be used to remove tarnish. For a quick tarnish remover place a piece of aluminium foil into a plastic bucket and sprinkle in 3 tablespoons of bicarbonate of soda. Lay silver on top of the foil and cover with hot water. Leave soaking until bubbles stop, then rinse and polish with a dry soft cloth. Store in a dry, airtight compartment lined with a tarnish-preventing cloth like baize or flannel. Wear cloth gloves when polishing silver not rubber gloves—the rubber will darken the silver. (See also page 72.)

GLASSWARE

Whether you drink champagne for breakfast or a warm glass of milk before bedtime, glassware comes in various shapes and sizes and can be very delicate or hard wearing but needs special care.

Clean delicate glassware separately from other dishes and use warm water and a mild detergent. Rinse well and dry with a soft, lint-free cloth. Use a plastic washing-up bowl to prevent chipping and wear rubber gloves for a stronger grip. A few drops of ammonia in the water will help remove ingrained stains. Use a soft toothbrush for hard-to-clean crevices of cut glass. Any glasses decorated with gilt or enamel should not be immersed in water or cleaned with ammonia. Dip them into warm water and polish with a soft, lint-free cloth. Crystal glasses dipped into 1 part vinegar and 3 parts water and then polished with a dry, lint-free cloth will sparkle.

Everyday glassware can be washed in the dishwasher but be careful of stems on wine glasses, and if the glass is thin, make sure you load it in carefully so as not to chip or break it.

Carafes or water jugs can be washed as for glasses but any stains can be removed by adding a few drops of household ammonia to the water and leaving to soak. Alternatively, fill with a denture-cleaning solution and soak overnight.

KETTLES AND ELECTRIC JUGS

These can be made of aluminium, cast iron, stainless steel and plastic. Wipe over the outside regularly with a damp, hot cloth to remove dirt and grease. Furry lime scale deposits will form inside kettles and jugs, and can be cleaned with a proprietary descaler. Alternatively, fill the kettle with vinegar to cover the bottom and the electric element, then top up with water. Bring to the boil and let stand for about 12 hours. Another method is to fill the kettle with water and place in the refrigerator overnight. The cold will work free the lime build-up. Boil the water and the lime will dissolve in it.

TEAPOTS

Tannin stains can discolour the inside of a well-used teapot. Spouts can be difficult to get clean so use a piece of old nylon mesh stocking wrapped round a pipe cleaner or bottle-cleaning brush (dampen with a little salty water for enamel or pottery teapots).

Aluminium Put a few apple cores into the pot and fill with boiling water. Allow to cool, then wash with hot water and detergent.

Enamel and pottery Fill teapot with a strong solution of 1 cup salt to 2 cups water and leave to soak overnight. Rinse with hot clean water.

Silver Drop little pieces of aluminium foil into the pot, add about one tablespoon of bicarbonate of soda and then pour on boiling water. Leave to cool and then rinse out with hot water and dry with a soft cloth.

COFFEE POTS AND COFFEE MAKERS

Coffee stains can contaminate the delicious taste of fresh brewed coffee. Always thoroughly wash coffee-making equipment after use and do not let dried coffee oil stains build up. As with kettles descale a coffee dripolator by running a water and vinegar mixture through the machine, or use a proprietary product. To remove stains fill a coffee pot with a strong solution of 1 part bicarbonate of soda to 2 parts hot water and leave to stand overnight; rinse thoroughly and dry.

Cappuccino machine Coffee stains create an oily scum, so clean cappuccino machines regularly to ensure they work efficiently. Clean around the espresso cup, the steam spout and where the coffee ground cup is attached with 1 part bicarbonate of soda to 2 parts hot water. Thoroughly clean the steam spout each time milk is frothed. Use a plastic scourer to remove any hard-to-remove milk. Also wipe away any

TIPS FOR WASHING UP BY HAND

Rinse and scrape all food debris from the utensils and plates and stack in order of washing—glasses first and then lightly soiled items.

Soak cutlery in a jug or pot of water (see Cutlery on page 26).

Soak dishes or pots if necessary to loosen cooked-on food.

Fatty or oily substances and sugary mixtures need warm soapy water to remove them.

Flour-based mixtures with eggs, milk, rice, pasta or corn need to be soaked in cold water to help remove any cooked-on particles.

Use only the required amount of washing-up liquid—a few drops in a sinkful of hot water should be enough.

Wear protective rubber gloves for non-slip handling of china and glass as well as to protect your hands from hot water and possible detergent allergy.

Only wash up when there are enough dirty items to warrant filling a sink with water.

Fill a bowl with clean hot water to rinse as you wash and place the clean items onto a draining rack. Alternatively, rinse by carefully pouring hot water over the rack full of items.

Do not waste water by rinsing or washing under a running tap.

Pour the rinsing water onto the garden, if practical, after finishing the job.

Let the items drain dry or dry with a clean tea towel before putting away.

To save water when washing up, wash dishes in a plastic bowl in the sink. Pour grey water onto the garden or pot plants. Strain first if there is any food debris.

coffee grounds left under the espresso cup with a damp cloth. Wipe over the outside of the machine with a damp cloth. Always follow the manufacturer's instructions for regular maintenance and cleaning.

Spouts   *see* Teapots

The kitchen floor

One of the most walked-on floors in the home, the kitchen floor should be covered in a hard-wearing, easy-to-clean material. It should be able to cope with all manner of things being spilled and dropped on it, yet look spick and span after it has been cleaned. Spills should be mopped up straightaway to avoid any slips and accidents.

Sweep the floor regularly. Use the vacuum cleaner's flexible hose if you need to get into difficult corners, or an old cotton sock on the end of a small, long-handled brush. Make sure all dust and food debris is removed before cleaning the floor.

Kitchen floors can be timber, tile, marble, vinyl and other practical (and not-so-practical), attractive coverings, all of which need special cleaning attention.

ASPHALT TILES

A hard-wearing surface still found in older houses. Wash over with a damp mop and mild detergent. Rinse off with a damp cloth and dry off with a soft dry cloth. Polish with a water-based emulsion polish if desired.

CONCRETE

It is preferable to paint or seal concrete floors for easier maintenance. Wash with warm water and detergent, rinse and dry.

CORK, SEALED

Never oil or wax this floor as a slippery and dangerous surface will be the result. To clean, mop sparingly with hot water but no detergent. Once a month mop with a mixture of 1 part methylated spirits to 10 parts of water, then rinse with clean damp mop. Buff up with a dry cloth tied over the end of the broom A sealed cork floor will require recoating after several years of heavy wear and tear; contact your floor specialist regarding resanding or resealing.

CORK, UNSEALED

A natural cork floor can have a waxed polished coating. Damp mop wash with no detergent to keep clean. Reapply wax polish every six months in heavy traffic areas to protect the cork.

GRANITE *see* MARBLE

LAMINATED FLOOR

Plastic laminate or laminated timber (strips of timber glued in sheets) as used in benchtops but a lot tougher to stand the wear and tear. Damp mop and wash with a mild detergent and warm water, rinse off and buff dry. Do not use any scourer to remove marks and stains as it will scratch. Use neat mild detergent to remove stains (see Benchtops, laminate, on page 16).

LINOLEUM

Still found in some old houses. Clean with a damp mop with warm water and detergent, rinse and wipe dry. Be careful not to spill water or to use ammonia or other alkalis on the floor as this will break down the linoleum and possibly cause it to crack. Black shoe scuff marks can be removed with white spirit or turpentine gently rubbed over the mark. Polish high traffic areas if necessary with a water-based emulsion polish.

MARBLE AND GRANITE

Sweep, then wash with damp mop with detergent and warm water. Do not use any acid-based cleaner to remove stains. Mop spills up immediately—oil and grease stain badly (see Tabletops, marble and granite, on page 50).

PAINTED TIMBER

Use a mild detergent and warm water on a mop which has had most of the moisture wrung out. Buff dry with a soft dry cloth.

PARQUETRY

Clean as described for other timber floors, depending on the finish.

RUBBER

Wash with a mild detergent and warm water. Do not use any spirit solvents or polishes on this floor. Fruit juices and oil-based spirits can react badly with the rubber so mop up spills immediately.

SLATE AND STONE

Slate and stone should be sealed to protect them from stains and marks and to keep clean. Wash with a mild detergent and hot water, rinse with warm water.

TERRAZZO

Sealed Damp mop with a mild detergent and warm water.
Unsealed Mop with a mixture of 2 tablespoons of washing soda in 4 litres of warm water. Mop dry with a soft cloth.

TILES

Ceramic Use a damp mop with a mild detergent and warm water; never use strong alkaline cleaners like ammonia.

Quarry   Do not wash a newly laid floor. Instead, wipe over with a mixture of 1 part linseed oil to 5 parts turpentine, and then sweep clean for the first few weeks. Wash older floors with a mild detergent and warm water.

Terracotta   A natural-looking floor covering that can show marks and stains. Proprietary products are available to seal terracotta, which should be considered if in a high-traffic area where spills are likely to occur.

TIMBER

Oil finish   Never use oil-impregnated mops to polish this floor as this can create a dangerous slippery surface. Sweep first, then clean with a damp cotton mop. Wash every month with 1 part white vinegar or methylated spirits to 10 parts hot water; wipe over the floor again to dry it. Spills can be mopped up with a dry clean cloth or paper towel. Sticky foods should be removed with a warm damp cloth and grease should be removed by first sprinkling with an absorbent powder such as talcum powder or flour and then wiping over with a warm damp cloth. If you wish to polish the floor use a liquid acrylic and spirit-based wax polish.

Polyurethane finish   *see* Cork, sealed (page 30)

Unsealed wax polished   Usually old houses have wax polished wooden floors which are not as easy to maintain as sealed wooden floors. To keep clean, brush off dust and debris regularly and wipe over with a damp mop or cloth to remove sticky or oily stains. Polish and clean regularly with a liquid acrylic and spirit-based wax polish. Be careful not to apply too much polish and only polish areas which need it, such as heavy traffic areas. This will avoid a build-up of polish which eventually will have to be removed.

To strip old polish off the floors use a proprietary stripper which is recommended by the manufacturer of the floor polish you use. Alternatively mix 135 mL of floor cleaner (see recipe on page 150) with 500 mL of household ammonia and 4 litres of cold water. Apply with a mop and let it soak in to dissolve the old wax. Use a sponge mop or newspapers to clean off the wax and remover. Reapply in spots where polish is stubborn. It is best to do small areas until you have covered the whole floor. Once the old polish is off, mop over with a damp soft cloth, then thoroughly dry the floor with a soft cloth.

If you have a problem maintaining a wax polished floor, consider stripping the polish off and having it sanded and sealed with polyurethane or oil. This will make the floor look great and much easier to maintain.

VINYL

Wash with a damp mop and mild detergent and remove black shoe scuffs as for linoleum.

Kitchen cupboards and pantry

Cupboards in the kitchen come in for daily wear and tear. Organise the storage so that the most frequently used food and equipment is handy to the work location, saving time and effort for everyone who uses the kitchen.

Cupboard doors Wipe regularly to remove sticky or greasy finger prints or marks (*see* Benchtops and work surfaces on page 16).

Cupboard shelves Clean out cupboards on a regular basis, rotating old stock and checking what needs replacing. Wipe over bottles and jars with hot water and vinegar. Shelves should be washed with hot water and detergent (add a few drops of household ammonia to remove grease and oil marks), then wipe over with a clean damp cloth and allow to dry completely before replacing contents. Place a few cloves and bay leaves in food cupboards to deter weevils and other insects.

Walls

Painted If particularly greasy and grimy wash with a mixture of 1 part washing soda, 1 part white vinegar and 2 parts household ammonia mixed with 16 parts warm water. Rinse afterwards with a bucket of clean warm water. Always wash from the bottom up.

Tiled *see* Benchtops and work surfaces (page 16)

THE BATHROOM

The surfaces and materials in a bathroom are similar to those in a kitchen. Wall and floor coverings, cupboards, fittings and equipment should all be easy to clean, waterproof or water-resistant and low maintenance. A major problem in some bathrooms is the lack of ventilation to cope with the condensation.

Mould

Mould or mildew grows in warm moist conditions and can occur on tiles and grout, shower curtains and bathroom walls, in cupboards and anywhere there is a build-up of moisture and where direct sunlight can not reach. In particularly damp spots you can put silica gel crystals, available from chemists, to help absorb moisture. Good ventilation is essential. An open window, an extractor fan or wall vent will help reduce moisture so that the growth of mould is less likely to occur. Steam is unlikely to fill the bathroom up if you fill the bath with cold water first and then mix in the hot water to the temperature you require. After taking a shower, always leave the shower curtain or door open to let the air circulate and wipe over the door and tiles with a clean dry cloth to help remove moisture.

Shower curtains   Scrub regularly with a soft scrubbing brush and a paste of bicarbonate of soda and vinegar, then rinse off. If they are washable, wash in biological washing powder (a washing detergent that contains enzymes and a mild bleach). Hang out to dry in the sun if practical.

Shower doors and walls   Clean mould from inside the sliding runners or at the bottom corners by brushing with white vinegar; use a small brush or bottle-cleaning brush. Wipe over the glass with white vinegar and rinse clean. Polish with chamois leather.

Tiles and grout   To remove mould wipe over with neat white vinegar. Leave on and gently scrub with a toothbrush on the grout, or nylon scourer on the tiles. Rinse off with clean water and dry.

If stubborn mould cannot be removed by scrubbing with vinegar, you may need to resort to a stronger cleaning tactic and use household bleach. Use in a diluted form first, 1 part to 4 parts water, in a water spray bottle; apply to the stubborn areas and leave on for about thirty minutes. Scrub, then rinse clean with warm water.

Make sure the room is well ventilated and if you are sensitive to the fumes wear a mask and eye protection.

Bath and shower mats

Rubber   Clean regularly to prevent slime or mould build-up. Wash with hot water and detergent and add a little vinegar (½ cup to 4 litres of water) to the water.

Wood   Scrub occasionally with a solution of vinegar and salt to remove mould or dirty marks. Rub in a little teak oil to keep it from splitting.

Baths and basins

Keep clean by wiping over with a cloth or a nylon net scrunchy ball after each use to remove tide marks left by soap or bath products like scented oils and herbal salts. Always add these products to a bath while the water is running to make sure that they dissolve and disperse. Bath crystals that have not dissolved can cause scratches especially in an acrylic or enamel bath. A stubborn tide mark will come off easily by wiping it with white spirit or household kerosene and then washing it off with hot water and detergent. Rinse with clean water and towel dry.

Acrylic or fibreglass   Never use a strong scourer to clean this surface. Use full-strength liquid detergent to remove stains. Really stubborn stains can be treated by sanding gently with very fine sand-paper and then rubbing over with a little silver metal polish. Buff up and the stain will have disappeared. Rinse with water. This method can be used on bad scratches.

Corian   *see* Benchtops and work surfaces (page 16)

Marble   *see* Benchtops and work surfaces (page 16)

Vitreous and porcelain enamel   Easy to keep clean with a light cream cleanser, or a paste of borax and lemon juice, rubbed on and then rinsed off with warm water. If you have a dripping tap, get it fixed and that will stop the blue-green stains! These stains can be removed by rubbing gently with the borax and lemon juice paste; leave it on for several minutes, then gently scrub off with a nylon scourer. Rinse off with clean warm water and buff dry. A very badly stained or worn enamel bath can be resurfaced by restoration professionals.

Cupboards

Bathroom cupboards can quickly fill up with odd bits and pieces and need a regular clean-out. Keep your medicines and first aid kit up to date. Safely dispose of any drugs that are past their use-by date or no longer needed. Make sure medicines and dangerous cleaners are safely out of the reach of young inquisitive hands—seriously consider child-proof locks. Any make-up or cosmetic creams that are never used should be sorted out and thrown away.

Mirror

Clean with 1 part vinegar or ammonia to 8 parts warm water and wipe over with a damp lint-free cloth. Polish dry with old newspaper or chamois leather. To keep the mirror steam free, wipe over when clean with equal parts glycerine and methylated spirits.

Shower

The shower may be over the bath or in a separate recess. The materials used to make a shower base or cubicle are usually the same as for a bath (acrylic, fibreglass, enamel or porcelain), unless of course the

Install an aerator showerhead to reduce water pressure and water.

Wash underwear in the shower by carefully trampling on items with your feet. This saves using the washing machine.

GREEN TIP

Use a mug of water for rinsing when cleaning teeth rather than letting the tap run.

shower head is directly over a tiled, concrete, slate, granite or marble floor. Clean the same way as you would for these baths or floor surfaces.

Shower head If a metal shower head gets clogged, place it in a saucepan filled with 1 part white vinegar with 8 parts boiling hot water. Simmer for about fifteen minutes and the limescale will loosen and the head will be bright and clean. If you have a plastic head soak it for twenty minutes in a mixture of equal parts of vinegar and hot water.

Taps

Brass and copper If they have a lacquered finish, wipe clean with damp wet cloth. Otherwise use a proprietary polish. If there are tarnish or verdigris marks, make a paste with salt and lemon juice and rub gently until the marks come off. If really stubborn, wipe over with household ammonia, rinse and dry off with a soft cloth and then polish.

Chrome Clean and polish with a cloth soaked in white vinegar or a few drops of water and ammonia. Use a toothbrush to get into difficult crevices.

Gold plated Wash with warm water and detergent and buff dry with a soft cloth. If tarnish marks occur, wipe off with household ammonia, then rinse and buff dry.

Stainless steel Clean with hot water and detergent, and wipe dry. Polish when dry with methylated spirits.

Toilet and bidet

Scrub the inside of the bowl and underneath the rim with a toilet brush every day to remove any unflushed deposits or stains and tide marks. Flush the toilet over the brush after you have finished. Use hot water and a mild disinfectant like lemon juice, vinegar or diluted tea-tree oil to keep the brush and bowl free from germs. To remove stubborn stains, spread a paste of borax and lemon juice over the bowl; leave for half an hour then flush away. Clean the outside of the bowl and regularly wipe over the toilet seat with hot water and detergent and a mild disinfectant.

GREEN TIP

Update your toilet system to a dual flush system that will reduce the amount of water when flushing the toilet.

THE LAUNDRY

The laundry may be part of your kitchen or bathroom or a whole room dedicated to the ancient art of laundering things from clothing to curtains. It will have similar work surfaces and floor coverings as the kitchen and bathroom. Make sure detergents and other washing and cleaning products are stored out of the reach of children and pets.

Clothes driers and washing machines   Wipe over the outside with a damp cloth. Wipe out the inside and rubber seals with a soft dry cloth to remove any moisture. About twice a year run the washing machine on a short wash cycle and add 4 litres of vinegar; this will remove any build-up of soap or detergent scum in the machine. Clean and/or replace filters regularly.

Laundry tubs   see Sinks in the Kitchen section (page 17)

Taps   see Taps in the Bathroom section (page 36)

THE BEDROOM

Although there are lots of different combinations of bedding and beds, keeping the dust and dirt at bay is not such a hard job if the bedroom furniture is easy to get at or under with the vacuum cleaner, broom or duster.

Beds

To get the best life from a mattress clean it regularly with the upholstery attachment of the vacuum cleaner, or brush it with a stiff brush. Air the mattress regularly and also turn it over at least once every few weeks. Most mattresses will have handles to make this easier, but if yours doesn't, make four handles out of cotton rope and stitch them securely to the long sides of the mattress. This will make moving and turning much easier, helping to prolong the life of your mattress.

Always use a mattress protector or cover between the mattress and the bottom sheet. This will absorb moisture and can be taken off and laundered with the sheets.

Spot cleaning   Attend to any spills as soon as possible; follow the instructions for spots and stains in the Stain Removal Guide on pages 112–136. Use a minimum of fluid when spot cleaning a mattress and if possible stand the mattress on its side to prevent it from soaking up too much. Use a disinfectant in the final sponge rinse. Let it dry and then if necessary use an upholstery shampoo. After cleaning, use a hair drier to speed the drying time. For urine stains try to air the mattress outside after cleaning or place in front of a window where sunlight streams in. Wipe the mattress over with a damp cloth dipped in warm water to which has been added a few drops of an essential oil—lavender, rosemary or other sweet-smelling oil.

The water in a **water bed** and the waterproof envelope containing it should be treated according to the manufacturer's instructions. The mattress and base may be upholstered and the top part may be removable and washable—check the manufacturer's instructions. Dust and wipe over the frame with a damp soft cloth.

Bed bases can be traditional sprung, divan, firm edge divan, solid top divan, slatted wood divan. To keep clean, dust and vacuum clean regularly when the mattress is being turned. Pull the bed out and dust and vacuum clean underneath and behind the bedhead if you have one.

Brass bed frames normally have a lacquer coating which only needs to be wiped over with a damp cloth. If the lacquer need replacing, clean it off with a suitable lacquer thinner. Clean the brass thoroughly and then recoat with lacquer.

Old iron-frame beds should be painted with a special iron paint as a protection against rust. Treat any rust spots by rubbing with steel wool dipped in paraffin.

Bedding

Sheets, doona covers, bedspreads and pillow slips should be washed regularly according to the manufacturer's care label instructions.

BLANKETS

Acrylic   Wash regularly by hand or in a washing machine in warm water. Rinse thoroughly and squeeze out as much water as possible. Hang outside to dry across two lines, for speedier drying and also to help keep the blanket in shape.

Cotton   Wash regularly following the care label instructions in a washing machine, or hand wash in the laundry tub or bath. Rinse thoroughly and squeeze out as much the moisture as possible. Hang outside to dry as above.

Electric   *see* Electric blankets (page 40)

Wool   Clean seasonally and check the manufacturer's instructions. Soak first then wash by hand or in the washing machine on a gentle cycle in an appropriate woolwash detergent. Thoroughly rinse, adding a cup of white vinegar to the final rinse. Drip-dry outside, hanging across two lines to maximise drying. Alternatively, take to a professional drycleaner.

TYPES OF MATTRESSES

Interior sprung, which have metal springs interlaced on a wire frame with wire across the top and bottom.

Pocket sprung, in which the springs are in a fabric pocket.

Posture springing, made of a continuous web of wire.

Foam, made of foam of varying thicknesses for comfort or low cost.

Padded layers, padded between the outer mattress covering with cotton, horsehair, hessian or foam, sometimes called a futon.

DOONAS

Cotton doona   A summer weight doona, suitable for people with allergies. These can be hot machine-washed. Some cotton doonas have a mixture of wool and cotton, follow manufacturer's instructions for cleaning.

Down, feather or mixed feather and synthetic filling   Air outside in the sun regularly. Check manufacturer's instructions for cleaning, usually by a specialist drycleaner. Blot up spills immediately. Shake all the feathers out of the stained area and treat with suitable stain removal method. Always use a cover to protect a doona from dust and stains.

Synthetic—dacron or microfibre doona   These are easy-care light doonas that are suitable for the warmer months, but as they don't breath like natural fibre, it is advisable to clean them more regularly. Wash in the washing machine following the care label instructions. (If too large to fit in your machine, have it professionally laundered or dry-cleaned. Alternatively, hand wash in the laundry tub or bath. Rinse thoroughly and hang outside to dry. Hang over two lines so it dries quickly.

Wool doona   These should be shaken and aired regularly. Treat as you would down, feather or mixed feather and synthetic-filled doonas.

ELECTRIC BLANKETS

Do not wash unless otherwise specified on the manufacturer's instructions; some have detachable controls and can be hand washed. Have blankets serviced and tested for safety each year, if possible by the manufacturer. Store carefully when not in use, preferably flat or rolled up in a pillow case. It's a good idea to hang electric blankets outside to air regularly, like other bedding.

PILLOWS *see* CUSHIONS (page 48)

QUILTS

Have valuable hand-stitched patchwork quilts professionally laundered or dry-cleaned. Wool quilts should be treated as for wool blankets (see page 39). If the manufacturer's instructions indicate that a quilt is washable, test first for colourfastness, then wash with a mild detergent. Hang out to dry, pegging between two lines.

UNDERBLANKETS, SHEEPSKIN OR WOOL

Check manufacturer's instructions. They can usually be washed gently either in the washing machine or by hand. Use a woolwash detergent and in the final rinse add a little olive oil (1 tablespoon to 4 litres of water) to keep it supple.

Other furniture

Clean and dust wardrobes, chests of drawers and other bedroom furniture following the same instructions for other similar furniture (see page 46). However, the inside of wardrobes should be vacuumed regularly to remove dust which accumulates on the floor. Wipe the inside over with a damp cloth dipped in lavender oil to deter moths. Dust the inside of drawers when cleaning out the unit, or putting away clothes at the end of the season.

STUDY AND HOME OFFICE
AND ENTERTAINMENT AREAS

These rooms and their furnishings are cleaned the same way as described for other similar parts of the house, but most homes these days will also have some high-tech office and entertainment equipment. The home computer does the accounts, homework and perhaps improves your bridge game. The fax and answering machine help to keep your social life in order and music enthusiasts will have CD players, tape decks, speakers and so on. And then there are the TV sets and VCRs, DVDs and portable radio cassette players.

Dust and dirt can damage all this equipment so it is wise to clean it regularly with a soft brush, cloth or feather duster. Control static electricity by wiping over with an anti-static cloth: this can be made simply by soaking a clean lint-free cloth in fabric softener, then squeezing out and drying.

Follow any manufacturer's instructions on special servicing or cleaning techniques, in particular inside any equipment. Always switch off and unplug equipment before dusting and cleaning. Never use a wet cloth to wipe over the machine as water will damage the electrical parts. It is best to turn off any electrical office equipment before cleaning.

Study or home office

ANSWERING MACHINE AND TELEPHONES

Dust regularly and wipe over with a soft lint-free cloth dampened with methylated spirits. Dust around the keys or buttons and the inside of the machine if necessary, with a soft synthetic watercolour brush. Replace the cassette tape(s) each year if necessary.

COMPUTER

Diskettes Store in a dry dust-free filing box.

Keyboard Turn upside down and shake out any debris that may have become lodged between the keys (eating over the keyboard is not a good idea!)

Use a soft brush to remove any dust or use a compressed air vacuum (available from photographic shops and office equipment stores) to blow out any dust or debris.

LCD computer screen Wipe the screen with a dry, lint-free cloth. Remove any finger marks with a damp cloth and dry with a lint-free cloth. Stubborn marks can be removed with a damp cloth rinsed in ½ water ½ methylated spirits. Dry with a lint-free cloth.

    Dust the casing with a dry cloth and wipe any stubborn marks with a damp cloth rinsed in ½ water ½ methylated spirits. Dry with a lint-free cloth.

COMPUTER MONITOR *see* TELEVISION SET (page 45)

FAX MACHINE

Wipe the outside of the machine with a damp soft cloth, and use methylated spirits to remove stubborn marks or fingerprints. Use a soft watercolour brush to dust around the keys. Open up the machine and remove paper, and wipe over the inside print head and cover with a soft-lint free cloth dampened with methylated spirits.

FLATBED SCANNER

Wipe screen clean with damp cloth or damp chamois and dry with a lint-free cloth. Dust the outside regularly and remove dirty marks with a damp cloth dipped in a solution of 1 part warm water and 1 part methylated spirits.

PHOTOCOPIER

Keep dust and dirt off the outside with a soft brush or cloth and remove grubby marks with a damp cloth dipped in methylated spirits. Wipe over the flatbed glass with a damp lint-free cloth, and remove grease or correction fluid marks with methylated spirits. The machine should be professionally cleaned or serviced according to the manufacturer's or supplier's instructions.

PRINTER

LED or Inkjet Follow manufacturer's instructions for care and maintenance. Keep free from dust and wipe over the casing with a damp cloth
to remove any dirty marks.

TYPEWRITER

Keep the typewriter in its cover or case, or cover with a cloth to
prevent dust and dirt accumulating in the machine. Wipe the outside
with a damp clean cloth. Remove dust and dirt inside with a soft synthetic watercolour brush or pipe cleaner. With an old-fashioned mechanical typewriter, wipe the letters over with a cotton bud dipped in
methylated spirits, or use a toothbrush if very dirty. Remove the ribbon
and clean round the ribbon-holder area. Put a sheet of paper into the
machine and type each key till all the ink and dirt has been removed.
Rub over the platen with a soft lint-free cloth that has been dipped in
methylated spirits.

For a daisy-wheel or golf-ball typewriter, follow the manufacturer's
instructions on cleaning. Instructions on how to oil any part of the
machine which is easy to reach will be in the typewriter manual.
Alternatively, take the machine to a professional office equipment
service store.

Entertainment equipment

COMPACT DISC, AUDIO CASSETTE AND RECORD PLAYERS

Keep the outside of this equipment dust-free and clean with an anti-
static dusting cloth and by removing fingermarks with a soft cloth
dampened with methylated spirits. Always keep the disc or tape
compartments, or the lid of a record player, closed when not in use. To
clean accumulated dust out of these compartments, follow the manufacturer's instructions; cotton buds covered with lint-free cloth and dampened with methylated spirits or special cleaning solvent as specified
may be useful to reach into corners. Use a head-cleaning cassette, as
directed, in audio cassette players.

To clean the stylus of a record player, flick any dust or dirt off the
needle with a soft watercolour brush. Dip the brush in methylated spirits
and then wipe over the tip and surround. Replace when the stylus is
worn, as it can damage the records.

All electrical equipment should be turned off before cleaning. Make
sure manufacturer's instructions are followed for general maintenance
and cleaning.

Home entertainment equipment can be a small or large investment, so it is important to keep it properly serviced and maintained to ensure a long and trouble-free life.

Keep pets off all electrical equipment. Cats have a habit of finding a warm spot which is often on top of VCR recorders or DVD players. Cover the equipment when not in use, or place in an area the cat finds it difficult to climb into!

Cockroaches love to hide in warm electrical equipment. Use cockroach baits near entertainment or any electrical equipment as well as throughout the house.

DVDs and CDs Store in their cases in a dry dust-free anti-static environment. Wipe over with a clean damp cloth moving the cloth out from the centre of the DVD and not in circular motions which may damage the DVD.

Long-playing records Keep fingermarks off the record by handling only by the edges. Dust with a proprietary record duster or brush. Replace in protective covers after each use.

DVD AND VCR

Keep in a dust- and damp-free environment. Use silica packets to absorb moisture if there is any possibility of damp or use a dehumidifier if the room is subject to condensation.

Dust the casing regularly with an anti-static cloth. Wipe the outside casing with damp cloth dipped in ½ vinegar ½ water or ½ methylated spirits ½ water to remove fingermarks.

If your VCR is not in constant use and is switched off, cover with a cloth when not in use to stop dust getting inside. Wipe the case with a damp soft cloth dipped in vinegar to remove fingermarks. Clean the heads with a special VCR head-cleaning tape available from electrical stores. Consult the manufacturer first for any special service requirements.

Video tapes Store in a dust-free anti-static environment. They are best stored upright rather than stacked one on top of the other to prevent pressure on the tapes.

HANYDCAM OR DIGITAL CAMERA

Follow the manufacturer's instructions for maintenance. Clean the lens, as you would for any camera, with a lint-free cloth.

LCD DISPLAYS/PLASMA DISPLAYS

Dust screens with a soft anti-static lint-free cloth and remove any stubborn fingermarks with a damp lint-free cloth or chamois dipped in water and mild detergent. Wipe over with a dry anti-static lint-free cloth. Dirty marks can be removed from the outer case with a soft cloth moistened with ½ water and ½ methylated spirits.

TELEVISION SET

Dust with a soft anti-static cloth and wipe the screen with a damp chamois dipped in water with mild detergent. Wipe over with a clean damp cloth. Dirty marks can be cleaned off plastic cases with a soft cloth moistened with a little methylated spirits.

OTHER PERSONAL ELECTRICAL EQUIPMENT

It is important to store this sort of equipment in a dry, dust-free safe place when not in use. Purchasing a storage bag or box is worthwhile. ***Walkman, notetaker, palm pilot, headphones, earphones, mobile phones*** Wipe the earpiece area with vinegar or diluted methylated spirits. Keep clean by wiping over with a damp cloth.

PORTABLE RADIO

Dust with a soft synthetic watercolour brush and wipe greasy fingermarks off with a soft cloth dipped in methylated spirits.

Chapter 3

KEEPING THE CONTENTS CLEAN

FURNITURE AND UPHOLSTERY

The living room, bedrooms, dining room, study and family room will all have similar surfaces, wall-coverings, floor-coverings and, of course, furniture. Unlike the kitchen and bathroom, which are high traffic areas, the spare bedroom or formal dining room may be used only every couple of months. They will not need the same high-level maintenance as the television room or entrance hall. It is a good idea to check these rooms occasionally as you might find the dog has taken to hiding his bones in the spare bed, the cat is sleeping on the antique lace table-cloth in the dining room and little Picasso has decided to paint murals in both rooms while you thought he was quietly reading his book.

To maintain a clean, dust-free room, the walls, ceiling and floors will need regular cleaning. Windows in walls and skylights in ceilings will also need to be cleaned if you want to enjoy the light and view. These may not be weekly tasks but it is important to know when and how to do it, and what professional services you might want to call in to do it for you.

HOW TO DUST

Dusting is the low-maintenance way of keeping the dirt at bay. If you can master this art then when you come to 'spring clean' everything it will not be such a hard job.

Always dust from the top downwards.

Dust brushes and wands   Great for carved furniture, small objects and ornaments, blinds, cornices and picture rails, upholstered furniture and curtains. A broom with a cotton sock on the end is handy to reach high cobwebby corners, as well as dusting the difficult corners of the floor. As with the dust cloths, soak the sock in paraffin and vinegar, rinse, wash and finish up with lemon oil. Dry off and keep in the cleaning box ready for the broom to wear. A fine feather duster which has been sprayed with a mixture of 4 parts water with 1 part liquid fabric softener and then allowed to dry, will collect dust from blinds, television and computer screens, glass-topped tables, video recorders— any surface that could be prone to static electricity.

Dusting cloths   Soft cotton—old tablecloths, nappies, sheets and clothes— is the best for furniture, but make sure all fasteners have been removed. Soak them in a mixture of equal parts of paraffin and vinegar. Squeeze out, rinse and wash in warm water. Add a few drops of lemon oil to the final rinse. Squeeze and then dry.

Gloves   You can wear cotton gloves to dust venetian blinds, piano keys and the legs of furniture with your fingers. Wash and rinse with a fabric conditioner.

Hair drier   An inventive but last resort to blow dust off in a hurry!

Paint brushes   Soft, long-handled watercolour paint brushes dust ornaments without knocking them over as well as cleaning ornate picture frames and furniture; they are terrific for venetian blinds. Rinse them with equal parts with lemon oil and water and then dry before using.

Vacuum cleaner   Your vacuum cleaner may have an attachment (such as a small soft brush) which can be used to dust upholstery, curtains, lampshades, blinds, radiators, and into the bottom of the wardrobe and bookshelves. A small brush on the vacuum cleaner is also very useful for dusting the books themselves.

Furniture care and cleaning

Furniture can be very costly, so it is important to know what it is made from and how best to look after it. Polishing or waxing furniture will protect the surface and make dusting easier, but much modern furniture has a sealed finish that does not require polishing. If you like a very shiny surface, look for furniture that already has a high-gloss finish—to polish a piece so that you can see your face in it would take a long time.

BAMBOO, CANE, RATTAN, REED, WICKER FURNITURE

If unsealed brush, dust or vacuum regularly. If really dirty, wipe over with warm soapy water, using a toothbrush to remove ingrained dirt in difficult crevices. Towel dry. To prevent drying out and cracking, this furniture should be thoroughly wet once a year and allowed to dry out naturally. Alternatively, wipe over with a little lemon oil. Cleaning with warm salty water prevents the furniture from yellowing with age.

CUSHIONS

Take cushion covers off and clean according to the fabric they are made from.

Feather and down-filled cushions should be dry-cleaned as washing removes the natural oils from the feathers. If you want to give them a regular airing hang outside in the fresh air for a day.

Polyester-filled cushions can be washed in a mild detergent and dried on the line outside.

Kapok-filled cushions should be dry-cleaned only, but like feather cushions put them on the clothes line and air them outside for a day.

LAMINATED FURNITURE

For tables, wardrobes and so on made with a laminated plastic finish, dust regularly and wipe over with a soft cloth dipped in warm soapy water. To remove greasy stains add a little vinegar to the water. Do not use any abrasive cleaner on this surface.

METAL FURNITURE

Aluminium   Dust regularly and wipe over with a solution of 1 part methylated spirits to 5 parts water. To restore lustre to outdoor furniture, rub over with fine steel wool, apply a thin coat of silicone wax polish and polish with a soft cloth.

Chrome   Dust and wash occasionally with a soft damp cloth dipped in warm water with a few drops of ammonia added to it. Polish dry with a soft clean dry cloth. Protect by applying a little silicone wax polish and polish with a soft dry cloth.

Copper or brass   A handle, lock or knob on wooden furniture may have a lacquer seal to prevent it from tarnishing, applied by the manufacturer. To keep clean, wipe over with a damp cloth and apply a little silicone wax polish. If the lacquer gets damaged it may be removed with a lacquer stripper then reapplied. If you don't want a highly polished look, just wipe over with a damp cloth and buff up with a clean soft dry cloth.

Polyurethane-sealed or lacquered   Dust regularly and wipe over with a sponge dipped in warm soapy water, rinse off and wipe dry.

Stainless steel   *see* Kitchen sinks (page 17)

Wrought iron furniture   Polish with liquid wax to keep rust away. Rust spots can be removed with steel wool and pure turpentine.

SPOTS, STAINS AND MARKS ON TIMBER

If you have a valuable antique piece that is marked or stained, seek professional help regarding restoration. Attend to any spills or marks as quickly as possible.

Adhesive tape   Gently apply a little household kerosene, then rub over with a soft cloth moistened with a mild solution of white vinegar. Dry and polish if necessary.

Burns and scorch marks   Gently apply a cream metal polish following the grain of the wood. If the mark has bubbled or blackened, sand with extra fine sandpaper. If you have to fill the mark, use wood filler then colour to match the wood with either shoe polish or wood polish.

Candle wax   Carefully and chip off any excess. Use a hair dryer, warm iron or hot damp cloth to soften up the wax. Rub over with an absorbent soft cloth to remove excess. Wipe over with a a damp cloth rinsed in a mild solution of vinegar and water.

Dents   Cover the dent with several layers of brown wrapping paper or paper bags, then place a damp cloth over the layers and apply a warm, dry iron to it. Try several applications until the wood swells and the dent disappears. Remove polish, then apply fresh polish and buff up. This will work only with solid wooden furniture. Damaged veneered furniture may have to be patched, a job for an expert. Badly dented antique or French polished furniture will need professional restoration. However, natural wearing over time may add to the beauty and interest of the furniture so don't feel you have to get it repaired unless it detracts from the natural beauty.

Heat marks and white marks   These can be caused by wet glasses, alcohol, some medicines and perfume spills. Blot with absorbent cloth and wipe over with a damp cloth. Polish with a soft cloth until the area is dry. If stain still remains, try rubbing a little toothpaste over the stain, or a mixture of powdered pumice with olive oil, or liquid car polish along the grain of the wood. Wipe over with a dry cloth and polish if necessary. Damaged French polished surfaces may need professional restoration.

Scratches   Using assorted brown crayons or shoe polish and a little petroleum jelly, rub over the scratch with the colour that matches, then rub along the grain with a mixture of 2 parts olive oil to 1 part vinegar. (See also tip on page 53.)

TABLETOPS

Glass   Wipe over with white vinegar and polish dry with newspaper.

Granite   Not as porous as marble; treat in the same way (see below).

Leather   Dust regularly and wipe over with a damp cloth which has had glycerine soap wiped over it. Wipe off with a soft damp cloth. Polish when dry with a soft cloth dipped in a little castor oil to condition the leather, and buff with a soft dry cloth. Use a leather polish in the same colour to restore any bad scratches. Marks from ballpoint pens can be cleaned off if immediately wiped over with milk. Sponge fountain pen stains off immediately with water and then apply glycerine soap as above.

Marble   Marble is very porous (granite a little less so) so always clean up spills immediately. To clean polished marble, wipe over with a damp cloth that has been dipped in water and mild detergent and polish dry with a soft clean cloth. Furniture beeswax can be used to bring up a good polished finish.

On unpolished marble, liquid stains like coffee, tea or wine should be attended to immediately. Try wiping over the stain with half a cut lemon dipped in borax powder or apply a paste of bicarbonate of soda and water. Wipe over afterwards with a damp cloth and buff dry with a soft clean cloth. If the stain is still noticeable, try a little hydrogen peroxide on the mark: apply it with a cotton bud then wipe over with a soft, warm, damp cloth.

For oil or grease stains on unpolished marble, rub over some corn-flour and leave for several hours. Wipe off with a warm damp cloth. Polish marble by applying a little whiting (finely ground chalk available from a haredware) to a chamois.

Plastic   Wipe clean with a cloth dipped in water and mild detergent. If required polish with a wax car polish.

UPHOLSTERED FURNITURE

Upholstered furniture can be covered in a wide range of materials and it is wise to use fabrics that are easy to keep clean and will not show the dirt, or to have covers that can be removed easily for cleaning. Some furnishings may be treated at the factory with either fluorocarbons which protect against water-based and oil-based spills or silicone which will protect against only water-based spills.

The best protection for upholstery is regularly dusting and vacuuming and plumping up cushions to shake out the dust. Always attend immediately to spills and stains. Be careful when vacuuming textured or ornate fabrics not to use an attachment which could catch loose threads.

The following fabrics are often used to cover chairs and cushions or made into curtains:

FABRIC	METHOD OF CLEANING
brocade	dry-clean
buckram	dry-clean
casement	wash
chenille	wash or dry-clean
corduroy	wash small loose covers of cotton corduroy, dry-clean others
cotton satin	wash if pre-shrunk, otherwise dry-clean
Dralon	wash and dry-clean upholstery
expanded vinyl	(used in shower curtains) wipe clean with a damp cloth and dry
glass fabric	hand wash in hot mild detergent, rinse well and drip-dry
lace	hand wash
linen	wash
moiré	dry-clean
moquette	dry-clean
nylon	wash
percale and chintz	dry-clean and press if the glaze has been starch wax applied. Wash if chemically treated.
rayon	dry-clean
sateen	dry-clean
satin	dry-clean silk and cotton, wash and drip-dry synthetic fabrics
silk	dry-clean; wash lampshades, first removing trim
taffeta	dry-clean
tapestry	dry-clean
velour	dry-clean
velvet	dry-clean

Use the appropriate upholstery attachment as recommended by the vacuum cleaner manufacturer.

Professional upholstery cleaners can clean furniture on site. It will cost on average $25.00 per item and if the furniture is covered in expensive fabric it is worth every dollar.

Fitted covers   Regularly dust and vacuum clean in all the crevices and seams as well as all the cushions. Plump up the cushions and check for stray earrings or coins that might have fallen into the cracks.

If an expensive material has been used, seek the advice of a professional upholstery cleaner before attempting to clean any part of the furniture yourself. Before using any upholstery shampoo make sure you test the fabric first for colourfastness. If you only shampoo one cushion or chair you might find the colour will fade and it will not match the rest of the furniture. Rotate cushions where possible on sofas and chairs so that they all will wear or fade at the same rate.

Check any care labelling information (see page 94) or seek advice from the manufacturer before attempting to clean. If there are any marks, stains or spills see the Stain Removal Guide on pages 113–136 for washable and non-washable fabrics.

Leather   Upholstery leather dyes are applied in two ways: with a pigmented coating or with an aniline dye. Pigmented leather resists water-based spills better than aniline dyed leather which is soft and more porous so that stains and spills should be treated immediately. Find out from the manufacturer or the supplier what sort of care the leather needs.

Dust regularly and vacuum into the crevices to remove dirt and dust. Wipe over with a damp soft cloth. If necessary shampoo the leather with saddle soap and buff up with a soft dry cloth. This needs to be done about once a year unless the furniture looks particularly grubby. Leather which is dark in colour can be conditioned by rubbing over a little castor oil about once a year; wipe over afterwards with a soft dry cloth. For pale leather, wipe over with petroleum jelly and then wipe it off with a soft dry cloth.. Leather can be polished with shoe cream in a matching colour if required or with a proprietary leather-furniture cleaner or polish.

Loose covers   Dust regularly with the vacuum cleaner or brush and only take covers off to clean when they begin to lose their fresh look. If washable, follow the care instructions on the manufacturer's label. Hand wash if you cannot fit the covers into the washing machine. Gently steam press with an iron any creases from the wrong side and use a starch spray which will protect the covers and make them easier to iron. Fit the covers back onto the furniture while still damp. Alternatively, take to a professional laundry or drycleaner.

Suede   Gently brush with a soft brush, or textured cloth such as towelling, to remove dirt and vacuum into crevices and along the seams where dirt can be trapped. The surface of suede can be damaged and flattened after a lot of wear and tear. Greasy stains can be cleaned off by rubbing ground oatmeal onto the mark with a cloth. Leave on to allow it to absorb the grease, then brush off and vacuum.

Vinyl   Dust with a soft damp cloth and vacuum in all the crevices. Remove marks with a cloth dipped in warm water and soap. Clean and polish the vinyl regularly with a vinyl car-seat cleaner.

WOOD FINISHES

French polish   Dust regularly and wipe dirty fingermarks off with a damp cloth dipped in white vinegar. French polished furniture will rarely need any polish; when it does, use a very little cream polish. Badly scratched or marked furniture may have to be professionally repolished. Use place mats and drink coasters, and never put hot or warm things on the table without first putting down a thick protective mat.

Lacquer or varnish   Dust regularly and wipe off any fingermarks with a mild white vinegar solution on a damp cloth. If required spray with polish and buff up.

Oil   Dust regularly and use an applicable wood oil every six months. Never use a furniture polish on this surface.

Paint   Dust regularly and if you need to

FOR SCRATCHES IN

Walnut—grind up some walnuts and rub into the scratch.

Red mahogany—use a fine paintbrush and paint over the scratch with a little iodine.

Teak—use steel wool along the scratch and then wipe with a mixture of equal parts of boiled linseed oil and turpentine. Polish with a soft cloth.

Deep scratches should be filled with wood filler then stained to match the wood and a similar finish applied.

THE FIVE BASIC POLISHES FOR WOODEN FURNITURE ARE:

Aerosol—normally a silicone polish which works best on hard surfaces.

Silicone cream—similar to aerosol polish and best used on high-gloss furniture.

Cream—often made up of wax, water and oil emulsion and best used on antique and old furniture.

Liquid wax—will contain natural and synthetic wax as well as a cleaning solvent.

Wax pastes—similar to liquid wax and may also contain silicones.

It is easy to make your own polish and there are some recipes on pages 152–153.

clean thoroughly, use a damp sponge amd a mixture of 1 cup of warm water mixed with ¼ cup of white vinegar. Towel dry and then if you require a shiny finish, apply a furniture polish and buff up. Fingermarks can be removed by wiping over with a cloth dipped in household kerosene. If it is an elaborate hand-painted piece of furniture check first to make sure you can use water on it. Most painted furniture will be sealed, but if it is a delicate decoupage or faux painted piece, dusting and wiping with a damp cloth may be all you need do to maintain it.

WOODEN FURNITURE

The enemies of wooden furniture are strong sunlight, extremes of temperature, abrasive objects and damp. Make sure your furniture, particularly valuable antiques, is not subject to any of these. When applying polish, wax or oil, start off in small circles and finish by buffing up in the direction of the wood grain. Be careful not to drown the wood (a very small amount will go a long way) and be prepared to use a bit of elbow grease—it's less costly than doing a workout at the gym and the result will be firmer upper arms and beautiful furniture. The best way to apply a liquid polish is with a pump spray bottle.

Wooden furniture should not be polished, waxed or oiled every time it is cleaned. If it is, it will end up dull, hiding the natural grain or colour of the wood. In most cases, regularly dusting and wiping off fingermarks is all that is required and polish can be applied about twice a year. If you make a habit of doing it at the change of seasons, it becomes easy to remember.

Dust antique and old furniture regularly and only use a non-silicone polish, if necessary, once a year to buff up and shine the wood. Finger-marks can be removed with a solution of 1 part white vinegar to 4 parts water on a damp cloth. Do not forget to polish or oil the underside of tables or inside cupboard doors—this will help prevent warping.

Periodically, it may be necessary to remove old polish or wax and start again. To remove dirty old wax apply 1 part boiled linseed oil (available from hardware stores) mixed with 4 parts turpentine. Apply it with a coarse cloth, wiping over until the dirty wax has been removed. Finish by wiping over with a clean cloth dipped in turpentine, then let the surface dry before applying the new wax. This mixture is also good as a 'soapless wash'—wipe thinly all over, then wipe off with a clean cloth and polish till you get a lovely shine. Old soft woollen clothing or an odd woollen sock make excellent polishing cloths for that final finish.

WINDOW COVERINGS

If you live in an isolated spot with only the birds and insects looking in, you may not need any window coverings. Wooden shutters, etched and stained glass and shady trees can cover the windows or provide shade. Window coverings help to insulate the house, making it warmer in cold weather and in summer keeping the sunlight out to help cool it. If you want to reduce the energy and time you spend on cleaning, only cover windows that really need it and on windows that are covered use materials that are easy to maintain.

Blinds

Like upholstery, some blinds may have a protective finish which inhibits mould, mildew and soiling; check with the manufacturer if you are not sure.

Austrian (festoon)   Dust regularly with a soft brush. Treat as for roman blinds, loosening the gathers and flattening out the blind before laundering.

Paper and bamboo   Dust regularly with a soft brush but never use water. As they are fairly inexpensive they could be replaced if really grubby.

Pleated paper   Dust with a soft brush and wipe over regularly with a damp cloth dipped in warm water.

Roman   Dust with a soft brush. If the fabric is washable, take down and carefully hand wash by sponging with water and detergent and then with clean warm water. Hang up in the shower or outside to dry. Otherwise wipe over with a damp soft cloth or take to the drycleaner.

Split cane   *see* Wooden slats

Stiffened fabric   Dust with a soft brush and if necessary wipe over on both sides with a damp cloth dipped in water with a mild detergent. Sponge rinse with a clean damp cloth.

Venetian   Dust along the slats with a soft watercolour paintbrush or feather duster. It is easier to wash these blinds when they are hanging up rather than taking them down to wash. Take a large pair of cotton gloves and stuff the ends of the fingers with cotton rags. Dip the finger ends into warm water and detergent and run the finger along the slats. Wipe over with a second pair of gloves to dry them off and buff them up.

Vertical   Dust regularly with a soft brush or vacuum with the upholstery attachment. Wipe over with a damp cloth dipped in warm water.

Wooden slats   Brush along the slats with a soft brush or feather duster. Regularly wipe over with a damp cloth which has been dipped in a mild detergent.

Curtains

The best way to keep curtains clean is to dust them regularly. Use a soft brush or the upholstery attachment of the vacuum cleaner. Long, heavy, lined curtains are best dusted regularly with the vacuum cleaner or soft brush and taken to a professional drycleaner or laundry for major cleaning. If the curtains are washable, take them down, shake them outside and then remove hooks and put in a marked container. Let down the hem and loosen the strings. Soak in cold water for a couple of hours to loosen the dirt, then hand or machine wash in a mild detergent. Hang outside on the line to dry. While still damp re-hang them with the outside edge to the centre (if possible) so that each curtain is rotated to even any fading.

Velvet curtains can be freshened up by rubbing them over with a chamois leather cloth wrung out in hot water.

Sheer net or nylon curtains should also be dusted or vacuumed, and washed regularly—once dirt becomes ingrained it may be too late to restore their original look. To wash, soak in detergent in a large laundry tub or in the bath and then rinse. Hang while still damp to let the creases fall out. Stiffen them by soaking a solution of 1 teaspoon of sugar to 1 litre of water. Net curtains can be brightened if they have gone grey with a proprietary nylon whitener.

Pelmets and curtain rails Dust and vacuum regularly, taking down, if detachable, when you clean the curtains. Use an upholstery shampoo on fixed, fabric pelmets at the same time you are having the curtains cleaned. Wood or plastic pelmets should be dusted when the curtains are down and wiped over with a soft damp cloth dipped in a mild detergent.

Clean the rails when the curtains come down to be cleaned. Dust with a soft brush and wipe over with a soft damp cloth dipped in a mild detergent. Metal or brass rails normally have a lacquer coating so dust with a soft brush and wipe over with a damp warm cloth.

CARPETS AND RUGS

Carpets, rugs and soft floor coverings are usually found in living areas and bedrooms. They are used for comfort, to fit in with the overall style or design of the rooms and in some cases to reduce noise. Wall-to-wall carpet can be very practical, adding to the feeling of space and warmth, but it also can harbour dust and dirt if not maintained regularly. As a major investment, it deserves high-quality care and maintenance.

Rugs and carpet squares and other mats can be changed with the seasons, or swapped from room to room. Oriental rugs can also be valuable investments and look stunning but they need special care if they are to keep their value.

Carpet

Carpet has two basic textures: loop pile or cut pile. These can then be divided into other textures such as multi-level loop pile, cut and loop pile, hard-twist cut pile. The best type of vacuum cleaner for removing the most amount of dirt from carpets and rugs is the upright style with motorised brush strips, full brush or agitator that beats the carpet as well as sucking up the dirt. A few barrel vacuum cleaners now have a power brush attachment, too.

These powerful upright cleaners, however, may damage carpets with a long or loop pile, or fragile antique rugs: a barrel vacuum cleaner will be less damaging to these finishes.

Vacuum cleaners will work more efficiently if the dust-collecting bag is emptied or changed when full and any material which gets stuck in the tube or in the brush or agitator is removed. Check this before you start to vacuum.

The best way to maintain and clean your carpet is to either:

- Vacuum high traffic areas only—hallway, stairs, living rooms, family rooms—each day or every other day, or
- Vacuum all the carpeted areas twice a week or at least once a week.

If you cannot vacuum under some furniture, have it moved regularly so that the area underneath can be properly cleaned.

For really efficient vacuuming move back and forward over each part of the carpet at least ten times. Play suitable music to vacuum to and perhaps practise the rumba, rock and roll or other dance steps as you push it back and forward. Swap arms and you will find it is very good for firming up the upper arms!

Use a carpet sweeper to do a quick sweep up, and dampen the rollers to pick up more dust.

Outside doormats are essential for people to wipe their feet on before they come inside, especially on wet days; encourage people to leave their shoes at the door. Another useful tip is to put a piece of carpet or a small mat or rug just inside every entrance to your home. Dirt will be walked in here first and stay on the mat, and will not be carried right through the house. A draft excluder on outside doors will also cut down on the dust that sneaks in under these doors.

WHAT SORT OF PATTERN OR WEAVE YOUR CARPET HAS WILL INFLUENCE HOW QUICKLY THE DIRT WILL SHOW

Plain colour, whether dark or light, will show any marks and dirt.

Patterns are less likely to show dirt and marks.

Berber—earthy tones with flecks of naturally pigmented wool—will disguise and hide marks and dirt.

Tweed is more colourful overall but disguises marks well, as does

Heather, which is similar to tweed and berber with small coloured flecks.

Stipple pile has two or more tones and depending on the depth of the colours used, can therefore disguise dirt and marks.

The most common fibres used in carpet manufacture are wool, acrylic and nylon or various combinations of these. When spot cleaning it is important to use any of the solutions suggested on pages 60–61 or in the Stain Removal Guide on pages 112–136 only on the indicated carpet fibre. Use the appropriate method for the particular fibre; if the carpet is a blend, follow the method for the fibre in the highest proportion.

WHEN AND HOW TO CLEAN CARPET AND RUGS

The amount of traffic a carpet carries, what colour it is, and how quickly it begins to lose that fresh look, will indicate when and how it will need cleaning. From a health point of view it is wise to consider cleaning carpet regularly to prevent a build-up of pollutants which can cause allergies (such as animal dander, dust and dust mites) that will get trapped in the fibres. Generally, carpet needs a 'deep' or restorative clean once a year and a 'surface' shampoo once every six months. If carpet is not regularly maintained, fibres will be damaged and its original appearance can never be restored. Any large carpeted area is best cleaned by machine, by either yourself or a professional carpet cleaner.

For a small area of carpet that needs a quick clean, use a coarse sieve or colander to sprinkle a mixture of bicarbonate of soda and cornmeal over the dirty areas and brush in with a soft bristle brush. Leave on over-night if possible, then vacuum.

A dry foam carpet shampoo or an absorbent compound cleaner are the best products to use if it is a case of having a go yourself, as neither leaves the carpet wet.

IMPORTANT STAIN REMOVAL CARPET CLEANING TIPS

Treat spills immediately.

Blot up the bulk of the stain with clean cloths, serviettes or paper towels.

Scrape up semi-solids with a plastic kitchen spatula, blunt knife or spoon.

If you are unsure how to treat a stain, call in an expert.

Do not apply a cleaning agent directly to the stain; always apply with a sponge or cloth.

Always start cleaning from the outside of the spot and move towards the centre.

Try cleaning a small area of the stain first.

Never scrub—gently dab, blot or rub.

Do not overwet the carpet. Wool will absorb five times more water than man-made fibre carpets.

EASY REFERENCE CARPET STAIN REMEDY CHART

Read the recipes for cleaning solutions on page 61 before using the table.

Stain	*Wool carpet*	*Nylon carpet*	*Acrylic carpet*
BLOOD	Cold water, then fabric detergent	Dish detergent, then ammonia, then dish detergent, then cold water	Water, than laundry detergent, then cold water
CHOCOLATE	Warm water, then carpet shampoo solution	Dish detergent, then ammonia, then dish detergent, then water	Laundry detergent, then water, then dry cleaning fluid
COFFEE/TEA	Warm water, then fabric detergent	Dish detergent, then vinegar, then dish detergent, then water	Laundry detergent, then water, then equal parts white vinegar and water
FRUIT JUICE	Warm water, then fabric detergent	Dish detergent, then then vinegar, then dish detergent, then water	Laundry detergent, then water
LIPSTICK	Dry-cleaning fluid, then fabric detergent, then water	Drycleaning fluid, then dish detergent, then water	Laundry detergent, then water
MILK	Warm water, then fabric detergent, then dry-cleaning fluid	Dish detergent, then ammonia, then detergent, then water	Laundry detergent, then water
SHOE POLISH	Dry-cleaning fluid, then carpet shampoo solution	Dry-cleaning fluid, then dish detergent, then water	Dry-cleaning fluid, then laundry detergent, than then water
SOFT DRINK	Warm water, then fabric detergent	Dish detergent, then vinegar, then dish detergent, then water	Laundry detergent, then water, then equal parts white vinegar and water
URINE (fresh stain)	Carpet shampoo solution	Water, then ammonia, then dish detergent, then water	Laundry detergent, then water, then equal parts white vinegar and water

Stain	Wool carpet	Nylon carpet	Acrylic carpet
WAX	Absorbent paper and a hot iron, then dry-cleaning fluid	Absorbent paper and a warm iron, then dry-cleaning fluid (for 3–5 minutes)	Dry-cleaning fluid
WINE, RED	Warm water, then fabric detergent	Dish detergent, then hydrogen peroxide/ ammonia, then vinegar, then dish detergent, then water	Laundry detergent, then water, then hydrogen peroxide solution, then water
WINE, WHITE	Warm water, then fabric detergent	Dish detergent, then vinegar, then dish detergent, then water	Laundry detergent, then water, then hydrogen peroxide solution, then water

RECIPES FOR CLEANING SOLUTIONS

DETERGENTS

Fabric detergent: 5 mL wool detergent and 5 mL white vinegar in 1 litre of warm water.

Dish detergent: 5 mL clear dishwashing detergent in 250 mL warm water.

Laundry detergent: 1 tablespoon laundry powder dissolved in 250 mL warm water. Do not use liquid detergent.

HYDROGEN PEROXIDE

Hydrogen peroxide/ammonia: 4 parts hydrogen peroxide (3% strength) with 1 part household ammonia (the foaming type which contains detergent). Use within 2 hours of mixing.

Hydrogen peroxide solution: 9 parts water with 1 part hydrogen peroxide (3% strength).

OTHER

Ammonia: Undiluted household ammonia (the foaming type which contains detergent).

Carpet shampoo solution: Follow manufacturer's directions.

Dry-cleaning fluid: Follow manufacturer's directions.

Vinegar: Undiluted white vinegar.

Compiled by CHOICE from information based on the Australian Standards for carpet cleaning.

Before attempting to shampoo the carpet yourself vacuum thoroughly and spot clean any bad stains or marks. Let the carpet dry. If possible, move all the furniture off the carpet. Apply the cleaner or shampoo according to the instructions. Let the carpet dry completely and thoroughly vacuum before replacing the furniture. If furniture could not be moved, or before it is replaced, put plastic or aluminium foil underneath legs to prevent wood, oil or metal rust staining the carpet.

If you decide to hire a hot water extraction machine to do a 'deep clean' yourself, it will cost up to $50.00 for 24-hours hire including the detergent, a defoaming liquid and stain remover. It will take a good five hours to do the job in an average-size home, not counting the drying time. Think about sharing the hire of a machine with a friend or neighbour and just do the rooms or areas that are in desperate need of a good clean.

The main thing that can go wrong is overwetting the carpet. If this happens, place as many thick dry towels as you can find over the area, standing on each towel as you put a dry one down, until most of the moisture has been blotted up. Place a heater and a fan in the room, and open all the windows and doors to let a breeze through. A professional cleaning company should always be called back if there is a problem, and is responsible for fixing any damage they have caused.

Do not move back into the room until you're certain the carpet has properly dried.

THERE ARE THREE MAIN CARPET-CLEANING METHODS:

Surface cleaning with a proprietary brand dry foam or liquid carpet shampoo, generally a do-it-yourself operation.

Bonnet cleaning or 'dry cleaning' (although it leaves the carpet damp), a general shampoo-and-rub by machine which is not a deep-cleaning application; this method is only available through a professional carpet-cleaning service.

Hot water extraction, also known as 'steam cleaning', which is the most powerful cleaning method and is used by professional carpet-cleaning companies. You can also hire this type of cleaning machine through local supermarkets and general hire companies.

Sisal, coir, rush and split cane floor coverings

All these floor coverings are made from plant fibres. Sisal is made from leaves of the agave plant which is then made into cordage and ropes. Coir is made from coconut husk and made into ropes and matting. Rush and split cane is usually woven. Most carpeting made from these fibres has a rubber backing which makes them easier to clean if they are fitted; dirt and debris become trapped between the fibres and the backing and can be vacuumed out. A backed carpet also keeps its shape better, and wet spills are easier to clean up.

They are hard-wearing but like most carpets very susceptible to water damage. Maintain by vacuuming dust and dirt out regularly. Spot clean any wet spills by blotting first, then applying an absorbent dry powder cleaner or dry-cleaning fluid. Check with the manufacturer before you shampoo or dry-clean. As with carpet, it is best to deep clean about once a year to keep the floor covering in good shape.

Because most of the plant fibre floor coverings are one solid colour, stains will show up more on the lighter colours.

Carpet squares, rugs and mats

Chinese rugs   see Oriental rugs (page 64)

Cotton rugs and mats   Shake outside and then either hand wash or machine wash. Check care label instructions and for colourfastness if you are not sure. Add some vinegar to the final rinse.

Flat-weave rugs (dhurries, kilims or Navajo)   Manufactured all over the world now, but originally made in India, Pakistan, Turkey and Morocco. Reversible, tightly woven and hard wearing. Vacuum as for carpets and if small enough take outside and shake or hang over the line and brush with a soft brush. Check for any care label or instructions before washing, shampooing or dry-cleaning.

Fur rugs made from animal skins   Gently dust with a soft brush or take outside and shake. Depending on the fur, try to clean it by rubbing an absorbent powder like fullers earth, french chalk or cornmeal into the skin and leaving that on for several hours. Take outside and brush with a soft brush or hang on the line and gently beat with a tennis racket. Repeat several times if necessary. Alternatively, wipe over with a damp sponge dipped in a mild detergent. Brush the fur with a clean brush and allow to dry. Take to a professional cleaner if at all worn, delicate or of great value.

Numdab rugs   Made from matted goat's hair from India, and are quite delicate so need careful attention. Vacuum regularly to remove dust and dirt and take to a professional carpet cleaner for deep cleaning treatment.

Oriental rugs or carpets   Made in Asian and Middle Eastern countries including India, Pakistan, Afghanistan, Iran, Turkey and China, these rugs are mainly handmade and should be treated with care. Vacuum as you would carpet, using only a cylinder or barrel machine suction vacuum cleaner. If the rug is small enough, take it outside and hang on the line, and dust with a soft brush. Spot clean as for carpets but test first in a inconspicuous area. Check with the manufacturer's or supplier's cleaning instructions before deciding to shampoo the rug yourself. If it is valuable or old and worn it is better to let an expert clean it properly.

Rag rug   Usually made of cotton therefore washable; check care label instructions if any. Test for colourfastness, then put in a pillow slip to protect it and machine wash, or gently hand wash. Dry flat to keep it in shape.

Sheepskin rugs   Shake outside regularly. If the rug has a backing, use an absorbent powder like fullers earth, bicarbonate of soda or french chalk. Sprinkle it into the rug and leave for several hours or overnight. Take outside and hang on the line, brush with a soft brush or gently beat with a tennis racket.

If the rug has no backing, you can sponge it carefully with a woolwash detergent applied with a damp sponge. Be careful not to wet the skin which can shrink. Carefully sponge rinse and add a little olive oil to the rinse (1 tablespoon to 1 litre of water). Hang outside to dry and when still damp brush the pile up. Alternatively, treat as you would backed rugs with an absorbent cleaning method or take to a professional cleaner.

Sisal or coconut rug   Shake to remove dirt and dust and vacuum both sides. Occasionally take outside and sponge with warm soapy water, then rinse with a garden hose. Leave outside in a warm spot to dry.

WINDOWS

Glass will not rot or fall out of a window if it is not cleaned and the only thing dirty glass will do is spoil a sensational view. Windows come in all shapes and sizes and can be made from different types of glass.

Whether you live in a five-storey glass pyramid or mountain-top log cabin, window are not difficult to clean as long as you hav the right equipment. If you have lots of hig windows which need a ladder, make sure it is one from which you can comfortably reach all the windows. If you do not have a suitable ladder, think about hiring a professional window cleaner to do all the difficult ones and you can maintain the easy ones.

The cleaning product can be a mixture of 1 cup of white vinegar with 4 litres of water or ½ cup each of vinegar and household ammonia to 4 litres of water.

When to clean Pick a time when the sun is not streaming in the windows you are cleaning—sun on the window will cause streaks. Obviously a cloudy day is best or clean the windows in shade first and when the sun moves round clean the others. It is best to do inside and out to get the best effect. Do not over-challenge yourself—do half one week and the others the following week. Or do the windows you look out of the most first and do the rest the next time.

How to clean   Start off at the top of the window and clean down. Apply the cleaning solution with the sponge, but don't have it too wet. Wipe across the window with the dampened blade of the squeegee, wiping it after every pass with the lint-free cloth. Follow with a rinse of clean water applied with the chamois. Polish off any remaining moisture with newspaper crumpled into a loose ball.

Small windows or stained glass windows should be cleaned with a damp sponge first, then wiped over with a clean damp chamois. Polish off with crumpled old newspaper. Delicate stained glass should be treated with

EQUIPMENT

two buckets

sponge

rubber window squeegee

clean lint-free cloth

chamois

old newspapers

care. Painted glass should be cleaned with a damp chamois but avoid harsh rubbing.

Window frames inside should be dusted regularly to remove dust and dirt. If the frames are really dirty, clean them before you clean the windows. Wash inside painted window frames with a sponge dipped in warm water and detergent, rinse with warm clean water, towel dry if necessary. Sliding aluminium windows and doors need to have their runners kept clear of dust and dirt, so vacuum these out before you wash them. Aluminium window frames can be polished with silicone car polish, which can also be used in the channels to help windows slide smoothly. Alternatively, lightly oil the running channels.

When cleaning windows check any putty that needs replacing, paint repair that might have to be done, or cracks in any of the glass.

Remove new paint marks from glass with a cloth dipped in turpentine if the paint is oil-based or warm water and detergent if acrylic. Gently scrape old paint from glass with a razor blade, but try not to scratch the window. Putty marks can be removed by wiping over with ammonia. Stubborn specks can rubbed off with a cloth dipped in cold tea. If you want to stop windows fogging up, rub over with a little glycerine after cleaning and the steam will just go away.

WALLS, DOORS AND CEILINGS

If you keep the dust level down on the walls and doors then when you come to wash them down it will be an easy job and you will not need any strong detergents. Ceilings should not get as dirty as walls and doors unless you have an inefficient fireplace that belts out smoke. Regularly remove old cobwebs and stop dirt accumulating in corners and nooks and crannies with a long-handled brush that has a towel or an old sock over it. Ceilings are difficult to wash so if dirty marks appear, clean them off or touch up with paint. Wash the whole ceiling when you are about to have a full paint job done.

Dust walls and doors with a broom covered in an old towel or use the vacuum cleaner brush attachment or a soft dry mop. Some rooms will accumulate more dirt and grime than others. Where there is a lot of through traffic and heavy use the walls and doors will show more marks. Fingermarks around light switches and door handles will be noticed first. Spot clean regularly, so that the rest can probably be done when it is time to paint or about once every two years if needed.

Always start from the bottom of a wall and work upwards as when dirty water runs down a soiled wall it can be even more difficult to remove; it will not, however, stain a damp wall that has already been cleaned. Wipe off any drips with a damp clean sponge. Wear rubber gloves and place sweatbands over the ends at the wrists to stop water running down your arms. Change the water in the rinsing bucket and the cleaning solution regularly.

Cork wall-covering This should be sealed both to keep dirt out and for ease of cleaning. Treat as you would for sealed cork flooring but be gentle—walls are not intended to resist the battering that floors get.

Fabric wall-covering Gently dust with a soft brush or damp cloth. Very difficult to wash, but spot clean carefully with a solvent suitable to the material. Check with the wallpaper hanger or manufacturer of the wall-covering on how to deep clean fabric covering.

Painted walls, doors and ceilings For water-based or plastic paints use an all-purpose cleaning solution:

> 125 mL ammonia
> 125 mL vinegar
> 2 teaspoons of borax
> 5 litres of warm water

Dampen one sponge with cleaning solution and wipe over surfaces, rinse off with the second sponge dipped in clean warm water and towel dry.

EQUIPMENT

two buckets

two soft sponges

a ladder or long-handled mop

dry absorbent cloth

Wash enamel painted surfaces with same solution but *omitting* the ammonia which could dull the paint.

Wallpaper, non-washable   Dust regularly with a soft brush or cloth. If the wallpaper is textured be careful not to damage it. Try spot cleaning grubby areas by dabbing powdered borax into the mark, then brush out. Alternatively, gently rub with a piece of bread rolled into a ball or a soft rubber eraser.

Wallpaper, washable   Dust regularly with a soft brush and wipe over with a damp cloth dipped in warm water and detergent. Rinse off with a damp cloth dipped in clean warm water.

Wood panelling   Dust or vacuum clean with a soft brush attachment regularly. Dirty fingermarks can be removed with a damp cloth dipped in a mild detergent solution to which has been added a little vinegar. Lacquered, varnished or waxed wood finishes can be cleaned the same as for wooden furniture (see page 49, 53 and 54). Painted wood panelling can be washed as for painted wall surfaces (above). Oiled or untreated wood finish should be dusted regularly and occasionally lightly wiped over with boiled linseed oil with a soft cloth, then wiped over again to remove any excess.

CLEAN AIR

We are all aware that there are pollutants in the air outside the home, but we sometimes forget that there can be many pollutants in the air we breath inside, and it is important to recognise the obvious and not so obvious pollutants. They include:

- cigarette smoke
- cooking odour
- dust
- fungi
- gas cooking appliances
- gas heaters
- household cleaning products
- personal body sprays
- kerosene heaters
- mould
- open fires
- pets
- wood-burning stoves

- building materials such as asbestos, particle board, plywood, rock and soil under the house
- newly dry-cleaned clothes or household goods (blankets, doonas, rugs, cushion covers)

The first most important thing is to make sure that the home is properly ventilated. Open windows and doors and, especially in an old building, keep outside and inside wall ventilation grills clean and free from obstructions.

Bare floors can help keep dust down when compared to wall-to-wall carpet. Rugs can be taken outside and aired and need to be regularly vacuumed or swept. Keep areas where pets like to sleep vacuumed and change their bedding regularly. Air pets' baskets or blankets outside regularly.

Install exhaust fans or window vents in the bathroom and kitchen.

Use an extractor fan or stovetop rangehood when cooking and clean regularly to remove grease and soot.

Clean and maintain heaters and other heating or cooling appliances on a regular basis.

Think about purchasing indoor plants to help clean the air. One plant can make all the difference in a small room. Think of them as your air-cleaning pets! Palms, ferns and weeping figs are just some plants that do well inside. Consult your local nursery about what's suitable for your area and the conditions in your home. Not all plants like light—they often grown in large, dense, sometimes tropical forests.

FIREPLACES AND HEATERS

An open fireplace should be cleaned out regularly if in constant use, so sweep out ashes and debris each day. Use the vacuum cleaner if necessary to get dust out of brickwork.

Brick surrounds   Clean with a sponge dipped in neat vinegar, then wipe over with a sponge dipped in warm water. Badly stained bricks should be scrubbed with a strong ammonia solution and rinsed with warm water. To prevent dust and grime entering brickwork clean thoroughly and allow to dry, then coat with liquid wax, or wipe over red-coloured bricks with boiled linseed oil.

Ceramic tiles   Wipe over when cool with a mixture of bicarbonate of soda and vinegar and water. Polish with a liquid wax to seal and prevent soiling.

Chimney   Wood-burning fireplaces used regularly should have the chimney cleaned at least twice a year, and flues on closed wood-burning or solid fuel stoves should be swept at least once a year. The resin from wood can settle in a chimney or flue and with the build-up of soot can create a fire hazard. Salt thrown onto the fire can keep the amount of soot down. Call in a professional chimney sweep to check the chimney out.

Electrical and gas heaters   Before the cold weather sets in, disconnect heaters and dust them thoroughly before using them. Wipe over with a soft cloth dipped in mild detergent. Use the vacuum cleaner to remove dust from grille fronts or between bars in radiators. The same cleaning routine can be carried out on portable gas heaters. Making sure the reflector is clean will guarantee a more efficient heater. Check electrical cord or gas hoses for deterioration and have the heater serviced as advised by the manufacturer and if the warranty has run out and the heater is several years old.

Fire irons   Dust regularly with a brush and to prevent rusting rub over the tips with kerosene. Clean any other metal pieces (see Metals below).

Freestanding metal stoves or metal parts   Wipe over with a damp sponge and mild detergent. to remove dirt and dust. If cast iron, wipe with vegetable oil to prevent rusting or use blacking or appropriate metal polish to restore.

Kerosene heaters   Wipe over regularly with a damp cloth dipped in mild detergent. Make sure the wick is trimmed.

Marble   Rub off marks with a paste of bicarbonate of soda and water or mild detergent and a soft scrubbing brush if stains are bad. Rinse with warm clean water. Wipe over with a soft cloth and buff up until dry.

Stone surrounds   To clean, mix powdered pumice stone to a paste with ammonia, rub over the stains and leave on for about one hour. Scrub off with a soft brush and hot water.

METALS

Metals pop up everywhere in the home—from the kettle to the door knob. Some metals have been mentioned already but this is a quick and easy guide to cleaning anything and everything a fast and simple way.

Dust all types of metal objects with a soft brush or cloth, then follow the cleaning and polishing routine. Some metals may have a lacquer finish applied by the manufacturer, which will make cleaning a bit simpler. Be careful not to use abrasive powders or scouring pads on soft or polished metals; stains and marks will usually come out with several applications of cleaning solutions. Metal polish will normally fill in any scratches. If a valuable piece of metal is damaged or badly stained, take it to a professional restorer.

Aluminium   Clean pots and pans with warm water and detergent and thoroughly dry with a soft cloth. Discoloured aluminium can be cleaned by simmering any acidic substance such as apple or lemon peel in water, or equal amounts of vinegar and water. Do not store food in aluminium. Aluminium furniture and door or window frames can be polished with car silicone polish which will give it a protective coating. Do not use any abrasive powders or washing soda on aluminium.

Brass   If not lacquered, rub with a paste of equal parts of salt and flour moistened with vinegar. Leave until dry, then rinse off with cold water and polish with a soft cloth. To clean engraved brass, scrub with a soft toothbrush dipped in household ammonia; rinse off with warm water and detergent, then with clean water. Badly corroded brass can be immersed in a solution of warm water and washing soda. Leave for about an hour and then rinse off.

Remove the lacquer from brass by rubbing with nail-polish remover or methylated spirits. Polish with lemon oil or use a proprietary brass and copper metal cleaner.

Never use metal polish on the inside of brass pots or pans.

Bronze   Never wash bronze, but dust over regularly with a soft cloth. Polish occasionally with a cloth dipped in boiled linseed oil and buff up with a soft chamois.

Chrome   Wipe with a damp cloth dipped in warm water and detergent; for difficult marks add a few drops of ammonia to the solution. Wipe over afterwards with a soft dry cloth. Use car silicone wax polish to restore scratched or rusted chrome, and to protect chrome in bathrooms or outside from moisture.

Copper   Use the same paste and method as for brass. Buttermilk, lemon juice or salt-and-vinegar paste all make great copper cleaners. Rinse and buff dry with a soft cloth.

Gold   Clean with warm water and mild detergent, rinsing in warm clean water. Polish with a chamois cloth. Be careful when cleaning gold plate which is normally quite thin and can be worn off if you are too enthusiastic when polishing.

Iron   Cast iron cooking pots should be washed in warm water and detergent and lightly oiled before being stored. Use steel wool and cooking oil to remove any rust marks. Wipe clean with a damp cloth. Protect outdoor furniture or other cast iron pieces from rusting by painting them with a rust inhibitor.

Lead   Small ornaments and old-fashioned toys made of lead can be cleaned by placing in a bucket with 1 part vinegar, 1 teaspoon of bicarbonate of soda and 9 parts water. Wear rubber gloves when handling the items. Leave for several minutes, then drain. Rinse well by pouring boiling water over the items and drain and leave to dry. Clean large items by wiping over with a cloth dipped in turpentine.

Nickel   Wash with a mild detergent and warm water. Polish with a soft clean cloth. Nickel will darken if not cleaned regularly.

Pewter   Antique pewter is more valuable if it is not polished; clean off dust and dirt by washing in warm water and mild detergent, rinse and buff dry with a soft cloth. Rinse pewter drinking vessels immediately after use as they absorb smells which will not come out. For any corrosion on pewter make a paste of flour, vinegar and salt, rub over the tarnish and leave for an hour. Rub off and then rinse in warm water. Try cleaning pewter with cabbage leaves or the cut tops of leeks—rub over the surface then polish with a soft cloth. This will give a soft lustre which is all you want with pewter.

Silver   Small items can be cleaned in warm water and detergent and polished dry. Rubbing silver will polish it, but Sheffield plate and Electroplate has such a thin coat of silver that harsh polishing may remove it—treat with care when cleaning.

If silver is tarnished, place a sheet of aluminium foil in the bottom of a plastic bucket. Put in 3 tablespoon of bicarbonate of soda, then the silver pieces. Pour over hot water to cover and let the silver stand for about ten minutes until the bubbles subside. The tarnish will lift off. Polish dry with a soft clean cloth. For larger pieces try this method in the sink. Line the sink with foil to cover the bottom and increase the amount of bicarbonate in proportion to the amount of water in the sink. Any bad tarnish marks that do not come off can be treated by making a paste with bicarbonate of soda, a few drops of ammonia and methylated spirits. Rub over the spots and leave on for about five minutes then rinse well and then buff up with a soft cloth.

Eggs, salt and harsh abrasives will tarnish silver. Use cotton gloves when polishing and drying silver to stop fingermarks getting onto the polished surface. Use a soft toothbrush to get into intricate pattern details.

Try not to overclean silver. If you use it regularly it will acquire a desirable patina which could be removed by cleaning. Use long-term silver polish about once a year if necessary.

Silver gilt   should be cleaned by washing carefully in hot water with a few drops of mild detergent and a few drops of ammonia. Do not rub it too hard. Rinse and drain dry, finishing with a gentle polish with a soft cloth.

Stainless steel   Wash in hot water and detergent, rinse and then thoroughly dry and buff with a soft cloth to avoid water spots and smears. Rub any stains with a paste of vinegar and bicarbonate of soda, rinse and dry. Do not use harsh abrasives.

Tin   Wash in hot water and detergent and because tin rusts if it is not dried immediately after washing, place in a warm oven to dry off properly. Rust can be removed by rubbing with fine steel wool dipped in cooking oil. Wipe over regularly with oil to prevent rust. Polish tin by rubbing with a cut onion followed by a soft dry cloth.

Wrought iron   Wipe over with a clean cloth. Apply a liquid wax polish to prevent rust or alternatively use a rust inhibitor paint. To clean off rust rub with steel wool dipped in household kerosene.

Zinc   Wash in warm water and detergent and dry with a soft cloth. Polish with a cloth dipped in household kerosene and buff with crumpled newspaper.

Chapter 4

OUTSIDE AREAS AND
GARDEN EQUIPMENT AND FURNITURE

T he phrase 'you can't tell a book by its cover' may be true about the
outside of your house. Falling-down, leaf-filled gutters, rusty old roof,
dusty dirty paintwork and an overgrown hedge might disguise an
exquisite palace inside, but just as you maintain the inside, the outside
area should have a bit of tender loving cleaning every now and then.

Regular maintenance will prevent deterioration and checking outside
regularly will uncover minor repairs rather than major ones! There are
professional exterior house-cleaning companies who will restore stone
and brickwork if the repair work is beyond your capabilities.

OUTSIDE AREAS

AWNINGS AND UMBRELLAS

Canvas   Brush off any dust or debris and use a stiff brush to scrub with
warm water and detergent, rinse. Afterwards sprinkle over with bicarbonate of soda to deodorise and help remove any stubborn stains. Leave
on for about five minutes then rinse off with the hose or bucket of
water. If damp or wet, allow to dry naturally before storing in a clean
dry spot to prevent mould. Remove mildew stains with a mild bleach
solution, testing for colourfastness first.

Metal   Dust off any leaves or dirt and then clean as for metals (see
page 70).

BRICKS AND STONE PAVERS

As the natural look of these for paths and patios is weathered, brushing with a stiff yard broom is usually enough. If mould or moss is growing on paths it can be treated by scrubbing a solution of mild household bleach (1 part bleach to 6 parts water) with a yard broom over the affected area. Leave for at least 48 hours before rinsing and scrubbing. Good air circulation and sunlight will help prevent the growth of moss and mould.

CONCRETE PAVING STONES, PATHS AND DRIVEWAYS

Sweep with a stiff bristle brush regularly and scrub occasionally with hot water and detergent. While the area is still wet, sprinkle over some dry cement powder; leave for about ten minutes then sweep off excess with a stiff yard broom. The wet area will absorb the dry cement powder and help give an overall cleaner look to the concrete. To prevent grease and oil drips from your car discolouring your garage floor or driveway, place a shallow metal tray filled with fine sand or sawdust under the engine area.

FLYSCREENS

If they can be removed take them off and clean with a soft brush to remove dust and cobwebs. Wipe over with a sponge dipped in warm water and detergent, adding a few drops of citronella or tea-tree oil to the rinse water. Dry in the sun and replace. If flyscreeens cannot be removed, brush the dust off the mesh and wipe over with a soft dry cloth.

GARBAGE BINS

Wash out regularly with detergent. Use a stiff brush to get rid of any dirt or debris. Rinse with a garden hose and wipe around the top with tea-tree oil or citronella to deter flies.

GUTTERS AND DOWNPIPES

Remove any leaves or debris from the gutters regularly. These will stop the gutters from working properly and also can be a fire hazard in dry hot weather. A plastic scraper and trowel can remove the mulch and then use a stiff bristle brush to clean the residue. Flush using a hose to remove any remaining dirt. Check downpipes for blockages and pour a bucket of hot water down them to help loosen any blocked dirt. Flush afterwards with the hose. Place a plastic mesh leaf guard over the gutter and downpipe entry to help prevent a build up of debris. Repair any rusted or broken gutters or downpipes. If you live very near the beach, regularly check the gutters for sand that may have gathered there after heavy storms and winds.

PAINTWORK

Depending on where you live, outside paintwork may need cleaning before you are ready to give it another coat of paint. Brush dust and dirt off first with a soft brush and then wash walls with a detergent or sugar soap solution. Apply with a large sponge and gently scrub any areas where the dirt is difficult to remove. Rinse off gently with a hose. When you need to repaint will depend on how well the paint was applied and whether it was good-quality weather-proof paint.

VENTILATORS

Clear away any debris that might block vents so that there is a good through-draught to ventilate the house and prevent dampness. Use a wire brush or bottle brush to wash the vent holes. Clear away any lawn or shrubs that are blocking underfloor vents. Window frames, doors, veranda and balcony railings
Dust off with a brush and if really grubby wash down with a mild detergent and soft sponge, rinse with warm clean water. Seal any cracks or gaps and replace putty in windows if necessary.

WOOD, SEALED

Wipe over with a damp sponge dipped in a detergent solution to remove dust and dirt. Renew sealer if the surface has weathered or started to crack.

WOOD, UNSEALED

Wipe with a damp sponge dipped in a detergent solution. Yearly, rub in a mixture of 4 parts raw linseed oil and 1 part pure turpentine to season the wood and prevent it from cracking.

GARDEN EQUIPMENT AND FURNITURE

BARBECUES

Metal cooking plates can be scrubbed with a wire brush and a little salt or sand while the plate is still warm. This will help to absorb grease and dirt. Wipe over with hot water and newspaper. Oil plates before storing or covering to prevent rusting. Barbecue grills should be cleaned by scrubbing with a wire brush and then wiping over with newspaper. The next time you heat the barbecue, old cooked-on grease and dirt will be burnt off. Brush out powdered charcoal or wood debris from underneath the grill or plates. If storing the barbecue, make sure all the parts are cleaned and oiled to prevent rusting. Place a waterproof dust cover over it or store in the garage or shed.

FURNITURE

Cane   Should not be left out in all weathers as it eventually may split or crack. Seal it with a quality outdoor lacquer. If not sealed, scrub down with warm salty water and leave to dry in the sun before painting.

Canvas or fabric   Clean as you would for canvas (see Awnings page 74). Metal hinges should be lubricated with oil or rubbed with petroleum jelly. Wipe over metal frames with a damp chamois cloth. Polish with a liquid wax polish to prevent rusting if desired.

Cast iron and steel   *see* Metals (page 70)

Wood, sealed   Wipe over with a damp sponge dipped in a detergent solution to remove dust and dirt. Renew sealant or paint if it is very weathered and has started to crack.

Wood, unsealed   Wipe over with a damp sponge dipped in a detergent solution. Yearly, rub in a mixture of 4 parts raw linseed oil and 1 part pure turpentine to season the wood and prevent it from cracking.

GARDENING TOOLS

Sort through and make sure that all the pruning and sawing equipment is clean and still sharp. Replace blades or get old blades sharpened. Wipe over or wash dirt off with detergent. Soak if necessary but be careful not to put any motor or electric mechanism into water. Use a wire brush to clean the blades of hedge trimmers. Dry all equipment thoroughly afterwards and lubricate to prevent rusting.

Lawn mowers   After each use, brush off dust and grass clippings and wipe over outside with a damp cloth; make sure the blades and rollers are free of debris. Take the machine to a professional lawn-mower service company for regular thorough cleaning and maintenance.

PONDS

A healthy pond has good filtration using either a machine or fish and plant life or both. It will not need emptying to clean unless fish become diseased or it is choked by too many plants and debris. Seek advice from an expert before emptying and cleaning the pond. Have the filter system checked and make sure any diseased fish are inspected by an aquarium expert or vet.

SAUNAS

Safety and hygiene are two important aims to keep in mind in maintaining this relaxing equipment. Follow the manufacturer's instructions on how to maintain and service the heating units and filters. Remove and lightly sand down the wooden benches and duckboards about twice a year, depending how much use they have had. The steam generally keeps the interior clean.

SPAS

Indoor and outdoor spas need proper cleaning and regularly emptying out. Follow the manufacturer's instructions on maintenance. If you keep your spa filled all the time, you will need a filtration system and a chemical treatment for the water—similar to. that used in a swimming pool.

SWIMMING POOLS

Maintaining your swimming pool is easy if you have the right accessories. A proper skimmer and filter, pool vacuum cleaner and leaf net are all essential to keep the pool clean. Chlorine or other chemicals are needed to kill harmful bacteria and algae, and to keep the pool water healthy. There are special test kits to establish the right pH and chlorine levels in the pool. Consult a pool doctor or local pool supplies shop if you have any problems with the filter or chemical balance in your pool. Regularly go over the pool with a leaf net to remove leaves and other garden debris which could clog up the filtration system. If there are algae growing on the pool walls or floor scrub over with a nylon scrubbing brush.

Keep the area round the pool clean by sweeping away leaf or plant debris. Prune back any garden near the pool if it overhangs or grows over any access to the pool. Nurseries are a source of helpful advice in selecting shrubs or plants to put near the pool which will not uproot tiling or drop leaves all the time. In dry weather or when the pool has had a lot of use, top up to keep the water level two-thirds up the skimmer box. Consult a pool doctor or your local pool supplies shop if you have any problems with the filter or chemical balance of your pool. There are special test kits to establish the right pH and chlorine levels in the pool.

Keep the paving and paths surrounding the pool clean by regularly sweeping them with a stiff yard broom. If any mould or algae is growing on the pavers brush them with a mild solution of household bleach, leave on for 48 hours and then rinse and brush with a stiff yard broom.

A concrete pool should be painted about every two to three years. Seek the advice of the pool supplier or paint manufacturer before attempting to do this yourself; it may be easier and more efficient to call in a expert to do the job.

TUBS

Similar to spas but usually made of timber, such as cedar. Clean regularly and follow the manufacturer's instructions on proper maintenance.

THE GARAGE AND SHED

Garages and sheds can be blissful places to potter around in and get away from the rest of the household! Dust can be swept out, dusted out and even vacuumed out. Check for use-by dates on garden products, glues and paints and phone your local council to find out how to dispose of out-of-date pesticides or oil- and water-based paints. Go through all your tools and see what needs oiling or servicing. You may find you have more tools than you own—return any borrowed tools! Place any hazardous or poisonous garden or household chemicals in a cupboard or chest out of reach of children, or which can be securely locked for safety. Clean out gutters and downpipes (see page 75). Clean windows and make sure a roller-door is free-running.

BICYCLES

Clean bicycles regularly to remove dirt, dust, mud and tar. Wipe over the frame with warm water and detergent with a few drops of ammonia added, sponge rinse with warm water and dry with a clean chamois cloth. Clean the spokes with a spray bottle filled with warm water and a few drops of ammonia. Rub over with a cloth to remove any moisture. Clean a leather saddle with saddle soap. Wash a vinyl saddle with a damp clean chamois cloth. Clean the chain and sprocket and gear mechanism with paraffin. Use a toothbrush or small paint brush to remove dirt and oil. Spray moving parts with a light oil, being careful not to get it on the brake pads and wheel rims. Remove tar, grease or rust by rubbing with eucalyptus oil. Take the bike to a professional bike shop for regular maintenance checks.

CARS AND MOTORBIKES

Keeping cars and motorbikes clean helps prevent paintwork and chrome deteriorating and rust developing, as well as improving the resale value. Tar spots can be removed by dabbing on a little tea-tree oil, then wiping it off. Sponge over the body with a mild detergent and then rinse off with clean water. Dry with a chamois cloth. Polishing will protect the paintwork and make the car look great. Use a polish that is easy to put on and polish off. Buff up with a soft clean cloth. Once you have washed chrome, dry thoroughly and apply a proprietary polish if you wish. Windscreens and windows can be cleaned with a damp chamois. Use a nylon stocking moistened with white vinegar to remove fly and bug stains rub over first, then wash with clean water and dry with a chamois cloth.

Inside the car have a rubbish box or bag in which to place accumulated bits of paper and other junk. Clean this out and empty and wash the ashtrays. Vacuum inside using the upholstery gadget on your vacuum cleaner, or take to a garage or carwash where you can hire a vacuum cleaner. Hand-held battery-operated vacuum cleaners are convenient but do not have very strong suction. Use an upholstery and carpet shampoo if the interior seats and carpets are very dirty. A foam cleaner is better than a dry powder shampoo. Follow the manufacturer's instructions. Alternatively, spot clean any bad marks with neat mild detergent, rubbing gently with a sponge. Leave for half an hour and then sponge rinse off with clean water. Use offcuts of carpet to protect carpet and cover seats with washable car seat covers if necessary or desired. Use a nylon knee sock as a filter over the business end of the vacuum if you think your diamond earring fell behind the seat! If there is any leather upholstery wipe it over with glycerine applied with a soft cloth. For vinyl upholstery, marks can be cleaned using a cloth dipped in warm water and soap or a vinyl car-seat cleaner. Dust the instruments and dashboard with a soft duster, then wipe over with warm water and detergent. Rinse with a damp chamois. Use tyre black on the tyres for a final gleaming finish.

PETS' PARAPHERNALIA

Our pets are important members of our family, but unfortunately they will never master the art of vacuum cleaning or shake out their own blankets, so care and cleaning will fall to you.

Whatever the age of your pet, little accidents can happen to the most perfectly housetrained animal.

Getting totally rid of odour is the most annoying after care problem. Pet vomit does not usually cause this problem, but urine and faeces present the worst odour problems after the deed! (See pages 60–61 for carpet stains and pages 113–136 for stain removal.)

Sometimes it is difficult to get onto the problem straight away, but once the initial clean up has been achieved, there can be some odour left in the spot. Animals will often return to the same spot, making it an ongoing problem. To deal with this, soak the spot with enzyme detergent and leave for several hours with an old towel or cloth over the top. Blot the area with fresh towels, sprinkle over bicarbonate of soda and leave for a few more hours, then vacuum.

A paper towel with a few drops of neat eucalyptus oil or lavender oil placed over the spot may deter the animal from going back. This odour remedy can be applied to hard floor surfaces and mattresses as well.

BIRDS

Aviary   If it has a fixed floor, sweep regularly and scrub with hot water. Clean and replace worn perches and nesting boxes; be careful not to disturb birds if they are nesting or have eggs or baby birds in the nests.

Cages   Clean out at least twice a week and wash all toys and equipment regularly. Wipe over the outside of the cage with a damp chamois cloth. If the bird flicks seed everywhere, protect the food container with a plastic shield which you can buy at pet shops. Alternatively, wrap the outside of the cage with long strips of nylon mesh (like shade cloth), enclosing the area from where the bird flicks the seed hulls.

CATS AND DOGS

Bedding or baskets   Shake bedding outside regularly and hang on the line to air. If washable, launder at least once a week to remove dander and dirt. Put a sachet of lavender, rosemary or citronella pot pourri in pet baskets to keep them smelling sweet and to ward off flies.

Bowls   Supply fresh water every day in a clean bowl. Wash food bowls in hot water and detergent every day, and rinse and dry. Stainless steel or pottery bowls are more hygienic than plastic which scratches easily and can harbour bacteria.

Kennels   Sweep regularly and wash floor, walls and outside with hot water and detergent, and rinse with clean water with a few drops of tea-tree oil added to it. Sprinkle pine needles or cedar shavings on the floor of the kennel to deter insects.

Litter trays   Remove solid matter from the tray daily and dispose of in the garbage. Empty litter, if very wet, every 2–3 days and dispose of in the garbage or garden. Wash tray with hot water and detergent, rinse, and wipe over with a few drops of tea-tree oil in water. Shredded newspapers or wood shavings are alternatives to proprietary brands of litter.

FISH

Pond   *see* page 77.

Tanks   To clean a tank, first carefully move the fish and some of the water to another tank. Empty the tank and wash in hot water. Never use detergents, bleach or steel wool to remove any algae build-up—use a plastic scourer or nylon stocking. Neat vinegar will also help remove any mould on an empty tank. Thoroughly rinse the tank in clean water. When adding new water to the tank, make sure it is the same temperature as the water already in the tank so that it does not shock the fish.

If you have tropical fish, check with your local aquarium about the safest way to remove the fish and clean the tank.

MICE, RABBITS AND GUINEA PIGS

Cages or hutches   If a hutch or cage has a fixed floor (concrete, glass or wood), regularly scrub out with hot salty water with a few drops of tea-tree oil. Regularly replace bedding—straw, shredded newspapers or wood shavings, and wash food or water containers.

Chapter 5

PRECIOUS ITEMS AND
PERSONAL THINGS

Maybe you have been lucky enough to have been left the family jewels and get to wear a diamond tiara on special occasions, or perhaps you have tucked up in the attic the Louis Vuitton leather luggage grandfather had when he set sail around the world in eighty days. Even if your really precious items are love letters tied with blue ribbon you might want to know how to clean and preserve them so that they will not fall apart when you cry into them. Here is a guide to the cleaning and care of items which could be termed precious and personal.

Alabaster Similar to marble; rub over with a damp chamois and spot clean any stains with lemon juice.

Artificial flowers *Fabric*: place salt in a plastic bag and put the flowers in the bag, heads down. Shake around to transfer the dirt to the salt. Alternatively, some fabric flowers can be washed. Test for colourfastness, then if the colour doesn't run, swish around in a mild detergent solution. Rinse in clean water. Hang upside down to dry.
Plastic: wash in hot water and detergent and then rinse in clean warm water. Hang up to drip dry.

Balls *Golf*: soak in a mild ammonia and water solution for several hours, rinse and then dry. *Leather*: wash with proprietary leather soap, dry and buff up with a soft cloth. *Tennis*: brush off any dirt and when dry rub over with a small stiff brush.

Baskets Wash in warm soapy water and scrub with a brush. Rinse with warm water and leave out in a warm or sunny spot to dry.

Binoculars and telescopes Clean lenses with a special lens cleaning cloth. Wipe the outside casing with a damp chamois cloth. Take to a professional camera shop for thorough cleaning inside and out if it has got very dirty. Protect from dust and dirt by keeping in a case or protective cover when not in use.

Bone   Avoid washing. Just wipe over with a cloth dipped in methylated spirits and buff with a dry soft cloth. Remove spots with a paste made up of whiting (chalk ground to a fine powder obtained from hardware stores) and methylated spirits. Bone can be bleached if yellowed: mix a little toothpaste and hydrogen peroxide together and rub over the stains. Leave for half an hour then brush off or rub off with a damp cloth. Buff dry with a soft cloth.

Books   Valuable books should never be stored in direct sunlight and there should always be a gap between the books and the back of the bookshelf to allow air to circulate. Place chalk or charcoal around to help absorb moisture thus preventing mould which is the book's enemy. Dust regularly with a feather duster or cloth, or even use the brush attachment on the vacuum cleaner. Remove all the books from the shelves at least once a year to thoroughly clean.

Leather-bound books should be wiped over with a soft damp cloth dipped in a mild woolwash solution. Use a soft cloth to wipe over them afterwards and allow them to dry thoroughly before placing back in the shelves. Rub a little castor oil into the bindings to condition. Wipe plastic or imitation leather over with a soft cloth dipped in a mild detergent solution. Buff dry with a soft cloth.

Cloth-covered books should be cleaned with an art-gum eraser or a stale slice of bread rolled into a ball. Gently rub over to remove marks and dirt. Wipe off mildew stains with a damp soft cloth dipped in a vinegar solution. Dust with cornflour to absorb mildew on any pages and leave for a day then dust off.

Damp or wet books can be dried in an oven on a very low heat setting. Pages can be dried by placing toilet paper between each sheet and leaving the book to dry flat and slightly weighted down. To prevent insects being interested in reading any of your books place lavender bags or cloves or bay leaves behind the books to deter them.

Bottles   Fill with water and detergent and add a few crushed egg-shells. Shake well and then use a bottle brush to swill them around. Rinse with clean warm water and place into a warm oven to dry.

Cameras   Unless you are a photographic expert, take the camera to a professional camera shop for a thorough clean. To remove dust from the lens use a camera blower brush, then wipe over with a lint-free cloth and proprietary lens-cleaning fluid. Keep the camera in a dust-free case when not in use to protect from dirt and dust.

Candlesticks To clean off wax place them in the freezer to harden the wax and then chip it away with a blunt instrument. Any remaining wax can be removed by pouring boiling water over it. It is best to use beeswax candles if possible as beeswax comes off straight away in boiling water. If you have wooden candlesticks, do not use hot water but try melting the wax with a hair drier and blotting with kitchen paper.

Chandeliers Don't try to swing on them to knock off the dust and cobwebs! Turn the power switch off, remove all the light bulbs and carefully dismantle all the pieces, remembering, of course, how to put it back together. Wash in a bucket of warm water with mild detergent and a few drops of ammonia. Rinse and dry with a soft lint-free cloth. Alternatively, leave in place and spray each piece using a water-spray bottle filled with warm water and detergent with a few drops of ammonia added. Wipe over and dry with soft lint-free cloth. Place an old sheet underneath to prevent dirty water dripping onto carpet or furniture, or if you are not superstitious hang an open umbrella upside down from the chandelier to catch the drips.

Clocks and watches The inside workings of clocks and watches should be cleaned by a professional clockmaker to keep them in perfect running order, but to maintain the case—treat as for glass, metal or wood.

Cloisonné Wash carefully in warm water and mild detergent. Rinse and dry with a soft cloth. Treat as you would fine delicate china.

Decanters *see* Bottles

Dolls Antique dolls should be treated with care as they are valuable, and any damage done while cleaning could decrease their value. Clean wax dolls by rubbing over them with cosmetic cold cream Polish afterwards with a soft cloth. Bisque dolls should be wiped with cotton wool dipped in a weak detergent solution. Take to a professional doll repair company if there is any damage to hair, body or eyes. Never wash a doll's hair if it is gauze-mounted with glue. Rag dolls should be cleaned according to the fabric and its colourfastness with either upholstery shampoo or dry-cleaning fluid.

Dried flowers These are great dust collectors so blow dust off with a hair drier. If you have to clean them further, place in a bag with salt and cornflour. Gently shake and then remove and blow again with a hair drier. Spray with hair spray to protect. Replace them if badly damaged, faded or very dusty.

Feathers Clean as you would for dried flowers. Some feathers can be washed in warm water then rinsed and gently blown dry with a hair drier.

Fur   Store in a cloth bag, on a well-padded coat hanger if the item can be hung. Never store in plastic. Shake out from time to time and take to a professional drycleaner if dirty. It is advisable to keep fur in cold storage in the summer months. Don't put it in the freezer but take it to a furrier who can arrange for cleaning and proper storage.

Gilded finishes   Picture and mirror frames, and certain furniture may have a decorative finish which looks like gold. This should be treated with care and dusted lightly with a soft watercolour brush. If the piece is valuable or antique have it professionally cleaned by a picture framer or restorer. Touch up with wax gilt (available from an art supply shop) any small scratches or chips but, as the colour may vary, it may be better to leave minor damage alone. Gently wipe over occasionally with a cloth dipped in methylated spirits warmed by placing a jar containing a little into a bowl of very hot water. Remove stains by blending an onion and dipping a soft cloth in the onion juice. Dab over gently and then buff with a soft dry cloth. Discolouration can also be removed with a weak solution of water and ammonia applied with a soft cloth.

Horn   Rub over a little petroleum jelly and then buff off with a soft cloth. Alternatively, use boiled linseed oil or olive oil.

Ivory   If kept in the light and not left in a drawer, ivory will not darken with age. Clean spots with whiting mixed to a paste with methylated spirits. Apply with a cotton bud. Wipe off and buff dry. Remove grease and dust with a soft cloth dipped in methylated spirits. Bleach yellowed ivory by rubbing over a paste of lemon juice and salt. Leave to dry, then buff with a soft cloth. Wipe over with a cloth dipped in sweet almond oil.

Jade   Dust regularly and wipe over with a soft cloth dipped in about 1 cup warm water mixed with 1 tablespoon of ammonia.

Jewellery

Amber and jet: wipe over with a damp chamois cloth, never soak in water. Remove grease by rubbing with a soft piece of bread.

Amethyst, sapphire and ruby: clean by soaking in 1 cup of hot water to which has been added 1 tablespoon of ammonia. Place the jewellery into the cleaning liquid in a bowl, swish around for a minute. Use a soft toothbrush to clean in ornate corners and clasps. Rinse well and polish dry with a soft cloth, or alternatively dry with a hair drier. Sieve the cleaning water before tipping it down the sink just in case a stone might have dropped out of a setting.

Coral, opal and turquoise: never wash, gently clean with a damp chamois cloth.

Diamond: wash as for amethyst but after cleaning dip in methylated spirits and then pat dry with tissue paper.

Emerald: a softer stone than diamond and can chip or crack, so clean with a chamois cloth and have professionally cleaned by a jeweller if really dirty.

Gold and silver: see Metals (page 70)

Glass beads: put them in a plastic bag and add 2 tablespoons of bicarbonate of soda. Shake about and then remove and dust with a soft brush. Buff up with a damp chamois cloth.

Jet: see Amber and jet (above)

Mother-of-pearl: wipe over with a soft cloth dipped in mild detergent. Rinse well and buff up with a soft cloth.

Onyx: wash in warm water and detergent, rinse and dry with a soft cloth.

Opal: see Coral, opal and turquoise (above)

Pearls: wearing pearl necklaces regularly will give them the best lustre. Wipe over with a soft cloth dipped in warm water and mild detergent or with a chamois cloth. Never clean with ammonia. Be careful not to spray perfume or hair spray on pearls as they will discolour.

Plaster and paste: brush over with a soft brush and wipe over occasionally with a soft cloth dipped in a weak ammonia solution.

Ruby: see Amethyst, sapphire and ruby (above)

Sapphire: see Amethyst, sapphire and ruby (above)

Silver: see Metals (page 70)

Tortoiseshell: see Tortoiseshell (page 90)

Turquoise: see Coral, opal and turquoise (above)

Wooden beads, brooches and bangles: wipe over with a damp chamois cloth and polish with a little olive oil. Rub in well and buff with a soft cloth.

Lace Delicate white lace can be soaked in a mild solution of cold water and borax. Wash afterwards in a mild detergent and rinse well. Dry between sheets of blotting paper and press flat. Pin it out to stop it from going out of shape when drying. Do not store in plastic bags but keep wrapped in acid-free paper to prevent discolouration. This isn't necessary for black or coloured lace.

Lacquered items (trays, boxes, lamp-bases) Dust regularly and wipe over occasionally with a damp chamois cloth.

Leather or suede, luggage, belts, handbag, shoes Leather and suede can be washed or dry-cleaned so check first with the care label or manufacturer's instructions. Before embarking on the cleaning, check for colourfastness. Leather can have a protective finish with a dressing of wax polish. This will help keep it supple. Suede should be brushed with a suede brush or with a piece of off-cut of suede. Mould can be wiped off with methylated spirits followed with a leather and/or suede conditioner. Dry wet items by stuffing them with newspaper and leaving to dry in a warm spot (but not in excessive heat as the leather will harden). Patent leather should be wiped over with petroleum jelly and then buffed dry with a soft cloth. Cleaning leather shoes regularly will keep them supple and in good condition, especially if you have expensive tastes in foot-wear. Apply a good-quality shoe cream with a soft brush, then polish off with a clean soft brush, followed by buffing up with a soft cloth.

Letters and old documents   *see* Paintings: watercolour paintings, prints and drawings (below)

Marble   *see* Tabletops, marble (page 50)

Needlework and embroidery   Lightly dust regularly and if colourfast wash in a mild detergent and dry flat between two towels. Press gently with a warm iron between tea towels Any old or valuable pieces should be cleaned by a professional upholsterer. Store as for lace.

Paintings

Oil paintings of any sentimental and/or dollar value should only be restored and cleaned by a professional art restorer. If it is something you have dabbled at yourself and you wish to clean it, dust well with a soft, clean watercolour brush. Mix a mild ammonia and water solution and use a small sea sponge to dab over a small area at a time. Afterwards gently wipe over with a soft cloth dipped in linseed oil.

Acrylic paintings: as for oil paintings

Watercolour paintings, prints and drawings: do not try to clean these yourself and take them to a professional art restorer if at all valuable. If any spots or marks appear on the painting or print, try rubbing it with fresh white breadcrumbs until the crumbs do not absorb any more dirt. Try removing stubborn marks with an artist's putty rubber. Watercolours, prints and drawings and other documents on paper (such as letters) if not framed are best kept stored flat, with acid-free paper between each, in a damp-free drawer and with an insect deterrent such as camphorwood balls or lavender bag.

Papier-mâché   Dust regularly and wipe off marks with a soft cloth dipped in a mild detergent solution. Dry off with a soft cloth.

Photographs   Fingermarks on photographic prints can be wiped off with methylated spirits on a clean lint-free cloth. These days specialist photographers and expert photographic shops can reproduce old photos which is a good way to show and preserve them. Try to put photos into albums regularly; this is the best way to keep them clean and to store them without damaging them. Plastic film and adhesive sheet photo albums do not stand the test of time, so put photos into albums with corner-mounts. Storage boxes and cover sheets which will not damage old photographs are available through specialist archival suppliers. Colour transparencies may suffer from mould if not stored properly, they should be cleaned by a professional photographic shop.

Piano   Have the piano tuned regularly and make sure it is not in a damp spot or too near a heater or fire or in bright sunlight. Dust the wooden case regularly and condition with a furniture polish if necessary. The piano keys should be dusted regularly and wiped to remove finger-marks and stains with a damp cloth dipped in methylated spirits.

Picture frames   When cleaning any picture frames be careful not to let any liquid seep between the glass and the picture, or onto the picture itself. *Wood*: dust regularly with a soft brush and if the surface is not sealed rub over with a soft cloth dipped in raw linseed oil.

Gilded: see Gilded finishes (page 86)

Plants   Indoor plants need their leaves to be kept dirt- and dust-free. Soft leafed or small plants should be sprayed with water or placed under a gentle shower. Larger plants can be wiped over with a warm damp chamois cloth. To polish the leaves of plants with a shiny leaf, wipe them over with milk.

Playing cards and board games   Clean paper playing cards by rubbing over with a small piece of fresh white bread rolled into a ball. If plastic-coated, wipe over with a warm damp chamois cloth. Clean a games board as you would playing cards and wash any plastic counters or dice in warm water and mild detergent. (If any of the pieces are made from ivory, bone or jade, see the appropriate cleaning methods in this section.)

Chess boards can be made from wood, marble or other materials so following the appropriate cleaning instructions listed for each material. Felt-covered boards should be cleaned by rubbing over with a paste made from french chalk (from the dressmaking supply shop) and white spirit. Allow to dry, then gently brush off with a soft brush. Alternatively, clean by sponging with a proprietary dry-cleaning fluid.

Shells   To clean and disinfect newly collected shells, put in boiling water with a few drops of household bleach added and simmer for about ten minutes. Dry and then just dust over regularly. Wash in warm water with mild detergent if dirty and greasy.

Soapstone   Similar to bone and should be cleaned by the same method.

Straw or cane   Dust regularly and if dirty sponge over with warm water and detergent. Rinse with cold water and towel dry and then leave in the open air to complete the drying.

Tortoiseshell   Wipe over with methylated spirits and then rub with a chamois cloth dipped in borax to polish.

Umbrella   To remove mildew stains, wash with a soft cloth dipped in vinegar, mild detergent and water. Dry outside in direct sunlight.

Vacuum flasks and drink flasks   Fill the flask with hot water and detergent and add 2 teaspoons of bicarbonate of soda. Leave for half an hour and use a bottle brush to swish around inside. Pour out and rinse well, turn upside down to drain and dry. Leave the top off to stop any mould forming inside.

Vases   To remove plant stains fill with 1 cup warm water, 1 cup vinegar, and a few drops of mild detergent. Let stand overnight. Add crushed eggshells and shake until the sediment has loosened. Pour out and rinse. See also Bottles (page 84).

Wood   *see* Jewellery (page 87); Picture frames (page 89).

CHILDREN'S EQUIPMENT

These days, there are many types of furniture and equipment specifically designed for children's safety.

DOORS AND GATES

These prevent children moving from room to room. These are usually made of sealed light metal, finished wood or strong moulded plastic. Dust regularly and wipe over with hot water and detergent and dry with a soft cloth.

PLAYPENS AND PLAY YARDS

These are usually constructed of sealed timber or strong plastic. Follow the same instructions for doors and gates. These need to be checked on a regular basis for wear and tear as they will be assembled and taken down regularly, and may need some maintenance on the joins and locks.

PRAMS, STROLLERS, JOGGERS AND BUGGIES

The huge variety of baby-moving equipment means that some are now manufactured using the high-tech, lightweight tough materials used to make sophisticated backpacks, luggage and mountain bikes! As these can often prove quite an investment, regular cleaning, care and maintenance is really important. Some babies and young children may spill or throw food or drink around, so a removable, washable inside is important.

Pram bedding or lambskin inserts should be washed as per labelling instructions (see pages 94–99)

Take the pram or stroller apart regularly and shake out any debris. Vacuum and dust both the inside and outside, and wipe over with a damp sponge with warm soapy water. Wipe over with a damp cloth and towel or air dry outside in the sun. (See bicycle maintenance page on 79 for wheels and frame.)

HIGHCHAIRS

Babies learning to eat solid foods can be very enthusiastic, which means you'll often find food debris all over a highchair once baby has finished eating. It's best to wash down the highchair after every use. Hot water and detergent with a damp cloth or household spray and wipe will fix the mess. Rinse off any detergent with a hot damp cloth. If the chair has a removable lining, hand wash according to manufacturer's instructions. Many liners are 100% washable and are easy to clean and maintain.

TRAVELLING COT, ROCKER AND CHANGE TABLE

These are usually made of easy-to-care-for materials like plastic, canvas, strong PVC and lightweight aluminium. Dust over regularly and wipe off any saliva or food stains with a hot damp cloth. Air mattresses outside regularly, and wash any mattress protector weekly.

CAR SAFETY

Capsule (birth to 6 months) To keep clean, wipe over regularly with a hot damp cloth and vacuum the inside if necessary when cleaning the car.

Car seats do get a lot of wear and need to be cleaned regularly as food debris may lodge in the seat, and little toys get wedged in the lining. Sponge over when necessary with warm water and detergent and air regularly in sunshine to dry.

Wooden cots and nursery beds The outside frame of these should be wiped over weekly with a hot, wet sponge to remove any saliva or sticky finger marks. (See travelling cot for bedding care.)

TOYS

These get more rough and tumble than other household goods and looking after them and keeping them clean will depend on the materials they are made from.

Plastic toys (small) can be soaked in a solution of one tablespoon of a washing detergent with enzymes in 2 litres of hot water and then rinsed dry. Scrub with an old toothbrush or plastic scourer to remove any stubborn marks.

Alternatively, if dishwasher-safe, place on the upper rack of the dishwasher and wash on a normal cycle.

Larger plastic toys that won't fit into the sink can be washed in the bath or wiped over with warm soapy water then rinsed off and air dried.

Bath toys may become mouldy, so wash in a solution of mild household bleach (1 part to 5 parts water) or soak in baby bottle sterilising solution.

Stuffed toys The method of cleaning will depend on the filling of the toy. New stuffed toys will be labelled with washing instructions. The filling of these toys will be similar to cushions, pillows and doonas and can be washed in the washing machine or hand-washed (see cushions page 48).

If the toy is suitable for washing, stubborn marks can be dealt with by soaking in nappy wash detergent. Always follow washing instructions first on any labels for colour-safe laundering.

Air them regularly by hanging stuffed toys out on the washing line in the sunshine.

Wooden toys If varnished or painted, sponge over with mild detergent and rinse with clean water and towel dry. If unpainted, wipe over with a damp cloth to remove dust or dirt.

Chapter 6

WASHING AND IRONING

Maybe the kitchen sink or the bathroom basin is your laundry, or perhaps the laundromat is your hangout. There are pick-up laundry services if you need them—just check the telephone book to find a service near you.

Old laundry tubs are now often seen filled with herbs in a rustic garden setting and the copper boiler, having been lovingly restored, is a prized, polished antique used to store wood or house a potted palm. The laundry mangle has been known to roll out pastry and pasta but it may now turn up in antique shops with a high price-ticket. Washboards will still be sought after by jazz bands for their percussion section, but most of us have moved on to the automatic washing machine and perhaps the drier, which is supposed to be the modern efficient way to do our laundry.

With the advent of automatic washing machines and driers, doing the washing hasn't necessarily become any quicker. The results may not be the best either unless we take a bit of time to read 'care labels' on clothes and other items which caution us and give strict washing or dry-cleaning instructions. Knowing the correct setting on the washing machine as well as the right washing product for the job is important, too.

Once the washing and drying is out the way, out comes the iron and ironing board. Maybe every item in your home and wardrobe has a 'non-iron' label, which would be rare, or you may like the scrunchy, unkempt unironed look. Ironing gives a certain satisfaction when done well. Clean, sweet-smelling, pressed cotton sheets are a joy to climb between and no one can deny the pleasure of unfurling stiff linen napkins that have been folded into an exquisite fan.

Basic knowledge of care labels, types of fabric and stain removal is important when you're sorting items to be washed. If you don't like washing, drying and ironing and are inclined to spill things regularly, you might want to choose fabrics that are easy to look after and can take the rough and tumble of your handling. Dry-cleaning can be expensive so always check for the 'Dry-clean only' tag when you're buying something.

CARE LABELLING INFORMATION

If you look carefully at clothing and other household textiles, bedding, upholstery and furnishings, you will see a label attached by the manufacturer which gives detailed instructions for care. This information explains the appropriate cleaning procedure for the fibre. Manufacturers will often put the most cautious instructions on care labels: if you think you can wash an item and the care label says 'Dry-clean only', proceed carefully (and at your own risk) and hand wash or gentle machine wash only. Care labels also warn against prohibited treatments (with the instruction 'Do not . . .'); if there is any possibility, for example, that an item might shrink or stretch, or that the colour may run if you use a particular treatment against the label's instruction, again you do so at your own risk.

The Standards Association of Australia sets down the terms and phrasing of the care labelling instructions and the terms that are used are easy to follow. A few examples of care labels follow:

A pair of black cotton jeans
Machine wash in warm water
Wash before wearing
Wash separately as dye might run
Wash garment inside out
Don't tumble dry
Don't use bleach
Dry-cleanable

White and orange spotted cotton shirt
Dissolve detergent completely before immersing
Gentle warm machine wash separately
Do not bleach
Do not tumble dry

Do not spot clean
Reduced spin or drip-dry
Dry warm steam iron
Do not dry-clean

Ladies 100% rayon casual blouse
Gentle cold machine wash in dissolved detergent
Do not bleach or tumble dry
Normal spin or drip-dry
Cool iron
Professionally dry-cleanable(P)(40 °C/105 °F)

Merino wool black jumper
Dry-cleanable
Hand wash cold inside out
Wash separately
Do not bleach or soak
Do not tumble dry
Cool iron
Store flat
Do not hang

CARE LABEL INSTRUCTIONS AND THEIR MEANING

Fully washable: wash, bleach, dry and press—no caution has to be taken here
Wash separately: wash with the same or similar colours, or wash on its own
Do not soak: colour could bleed or material could weaken if left wet or soaking
Do not bleach: do not use any type of bleach
Do not wring: fabric may be damaged or permanently crease, so do not wring by machine or hand
Do not use bleach, detergents or enzyme washing products: this instruction is for sheepskin products
Cold wash: wash in water supply cold water
Warm wash: hand hot water 40 °C to be used
Hot wash: use water temperature to 60 °C
Gentle machine wash: low washing speed action
Machine wash: normal machine wash setting action, no special treatment
Hand wash: hand wash with moderate rubbing and squeezing

Short machine wash: a quick gentle machine wash cycle without too much rinsing, agitation, or spinning

Drip-dry: hang when wet, do not wring

Dry in shade: hang out of direct sunlight

Dry flat in shade: dry on a flat surface out of direct sunlight

Dry away from direct heat: do not dry over a radiator or near a fireplace or electric fire

May be tumble dried hot/warm/cold: Dry in tumble drier on hot/warm/cold setting only

Hand wash separately: wash alone or with similar colours

DRY-CLEANING

The item can be dry-cleaned

⊗ The item cannot be dry-cleaned

Ⓐ The item can be dry-cleaned in all dry-cleaning solvents

Ⓟ The items can be cleaned in perchlorethylene, white spirit or fluorocarbons (the last two phased out in Australia in 1996).

Ⓟ The items are 'sensitive' and must be dry-cleaned as per P but with strict limitation on either the amount of water and mechanical action or drying temperature or both. If the drying temperature is to be limited, the temperature should be illustrated.

Ⓕ Dry-clean the items in white spirit or trichlorotrifluorethane only

Ⓕ The items are 'sensitive' and must be dry-cleaned in accordance with Ⓕ but with strict limitations on either the amount of water and mechanical action or drying temperature or both. If the drying temperature is to be limited, the temperature should be illustrated.

WHAT FABRICS ARE MADE FROM

Care labels will tell you what the item is made from but if you have no idea what polyester or rayon is or whether it is a natural or man-made fibre, the following will give a little guidance.

Natural fabrics

There are the four main natural fabrics which are comfortable to wear and if looked after properly can last a lifetime or be passed down from generation to generation.

Cotton Made from the seed hair of the cotton plant which matures to a cotton boll in about six months. It is absorbent, comfortable and cool to wear in a hot climate. Wrinkles easily but irons well and is moth safe. Some cotton fabrics are buckram, canvas, chintz, corduroy, denim, gaberdine, jersey, lace, lawn, muslin, organdie, percale, poplin, seersucker, ticking, voile.

Treatment Cotton fabrics can be machine washed and dried but always check the care label first. Wash similar colours together, especially red and dark colours; check for colourfastness before washing if not sure. Fine delicate cottons should be treated with care. White cottons can be bleached and also washed in very hot temperatures.

Linen Made from the stems of the flax plant and similar in many ways to cotton, linen is not as strong or resilient as cotton and does not hold dyes as well.

Treatment Some linens can be machine washed and dried, as well as dry-cleaned. It wrinkles easily so iron when damp. Always check for colourfastness and if not sure do not wash on high temperatures unless specified by the care label.

Silk Spun by the larva of a moth which makes the silk thread from secretions from its head, silk is the strongest of all the natural fibres and is usually wrinkle resistant and elastic, holds its shape well and is cool and light to wear in hot climates. Strong sunlight can weaken the fabric and fade the colour. When the natural gum is not cleaned from the fibre, the fabric is called raw silk. Shantung, pongee and tussah are all unevenly woven silks and are usually not dyed. A few special silk fabrics which are used for evening wear and furnishings include chiffon, crepe, georgette, grosgrain, moire, organza, satin, taffeta, voile. Vegetable dyes are often used to colour silk so it is important to check for colourfastness. Dry-cleaning will not fade vegetable dyes.

Treatment Strong, firmly woven silk can stand washing better than a flimsy silk fabric. Gentle machine or hand wash and dry flat in the shade; do not wring or twist. Always test for colourfastness first, then wash in cold water and with the final rinse add 1 tablespoon of white vinegar to 4 litres of water. Iron silk while it is still damp. Never soak or wash in a enzyme detergent. Use a gentle woolwash soapless detergent to hand wash delicate silk. Perfume, strong deodorant or perspiration can damage the silk fibres if left on the fabric, so always wash after wearing. Do not attempt to spot clean stains, which can weaken the fabric and cause permanent marks. Always take to a dry-cleaning expert—it will be worth the cost.

Wool Made from the fleece of animals, wool is wrinkle resistant, water repellent, and stain and soil resistant. It is warm and it retains colour well.

'Virgin wool' is made from wool that has not been made up into anything before and it may be softer than other woollens.

Types of wool fabrics can be jersey, gaberdine, crepe, twills and broadcloth.

Treatment   Unless specified, wool should be dry-cleaned only. Some items may be labelled 'Washable' so hand wash carefully in cold water with a mild woolwash mix, roll in a towel to remove excess moisture and place on a dry towel and lay flat to dry to keep the item in shape. If labelled 'Machine washable', wash on the gentlest wool setting. Flat dry on a towel. Store carefully and protect from moth damage with a herbal lavender bag or cedarwood blocks.

Types of wool include:

- alpaca—made from alpaca goats
- angora—made from the fur of angora rabbits
- camelhair—made from camels' hair
- cashmere—made from the soft underhair of high-mountain Asian goats
- lambswool—from lambs sheared at eight to nine months
- llama—made from llamas
- mohair—made from angora goats

Man-made fabrics

Often less expensive than natural fibres, man-made fibres are normally easy to care for, wrinkle resistant, mothproof, hold dyes really well and can be made to look and feel like natural fabrics. They do not 'breathe' in the same way as natural fibres and therefore can be uncomfortable to wear in warm climates. Some fibres are heat sensitive and should not be left to dry near fireplaces or radiators. Unfortunately man-made fabrics are not as stain resistant as natural fibres and may require more care when washing to remove marks.

Today many manufacturers blend man-made and natural fibres to obtain good points from one and minimise bad points of others; for example, to help an article maintain its shape, to cut down on costs, to improve durability or for ease of maintenance. Care labelling should list the materials the article is made of in order, for example—54% Linen 24% Cotton 22% Viscose. There is a large and growing range of man-made fibres, and some of the most common ones follow.

Acetate   This material drapes well and is often made into satins or used for lining.

Treatment   Dry-clean only unless otherwise specified. If labelled 'Washable', wash in cold water as for delicates.

Acrylic (sometimes known as orlon)   Resembles wool and is often blended with wool.

Treatment   Hand wash or gentle machine wash; it can pill if treated roughly, so turn the garment inside out before washing. Drips dry fast and tends not to wrinkle.

Mod acrylic   Often used for stuffing toys. It is lightweight, bulky and warm and is used for fake fur.

Treatment   Hand wash or gentle machine wash.

Nylon   Strong and lightweight, but white or pale-coloured articles can yellow if dried in direct sunlight. It can also fade and look flat and grey. Nylon does tend to attract dyes from other articles when washed together.

Treatment   Hand wash separately or gentle machine wash with similar coloured articles and fibres. Wash items after every wear as nylon is hard to keep clean once badly soiled.

Polyester   Keeps its shape well and resists shrinking and wrinkling. A tough durable fabric which can handle rough treatment. Dries quickly, lightweight and fade-resistant, but can pill easily and attract oil stains and soiling from other items in the wash. When blended with natural fibres, however, its good qualities enhance their maintenance and durability.

Treatment   Hand wash or gentle machine wash.

Rayon (also known as viscose)   Originally known as 'synthetic silk', it is lightweight, holds dyes well, very strong when dry, but weakens and is flimsy when wet. Wrinkles and does not hold its shape well.

Treatment   Wash by hand or if machine washable use gentle wash setting.

Spandex, Elastane, Lycra   Fabrics used for swimwear, other sportswear, underwear, etc, when an article needs elasticity to hold its shape. Usually blended with cotton, acetate or wool.

Treatment   Hand wash or gentle machine wash. Wash as for wool if you want to get the longest life out of the fabric.

TIPS ON SORTING OUT THE LAUNDRY

Most clothes unless they are really soiled will need only a cold wash.

Heavily soiled clothes need pre-soaking and then washing on a setting applicable to the fabric.

Colours that may run or bleed should be washed with the same or similar coloured articles.

Light-coloured clothes should be washed together.

Lint-depositing items should be washed together or with items that do not attract lint.

Empty all pockets, undo any zippers and all buttons.

Any trim, hooks and eyes, or buttons which could cause damage to other items in the wash, should be fastened, turned to the inside, or removed.

Belts should be tied so they don't tangle up all the washing, apron strings should be tied in a bow.

Delicate items should be washed in a laundry mesh bag or put in a pillow slip.

Blended fabrics should be cleaned according to the major fibre content. Check the label for details. For example, if an item is 50% polyester, 40% cotton 10% Spandex, treat it as you would polyester.

Clothing such as sweatshirts and tracksuits that are likely to pill should be turned inside out before washing.

Check for loose buttons and remove or sew back on before washing.

Mend any rips as they will only deteriorate during washing.

If you suspect an item might not be colourfast, check before washing it: find a spot like the hem or another area which is inconspicuous and wet it with cold water. Place a piece of white cloth—an old handkerchief or nappy would do—on the top and blot the area with a piece of white cloth. If there is any colour transference, wash the item separately or have it dry-cleaned.

Some articles may not be colourfast when using bleach. Test by dabbing with a cotton bud dipped in 1 part bleach to 3 parts warm water. Dab dry and if the colour comes out do not bleach.

To set colour, rinse the item in 1 litre of cold water to which has been added 3 tablespoons of salt and 1 cup of vinegar.

LAUNDRY CARE TIPS

Hand washing

- Fill a bowl, bucket or tub with water and make sure the washing product is completely dissolved.
- Use a product specifically designed for gentle hand washing.
- Check care label and only soak clothes for a short time to loosen dirt; badly soiled items can be soaked for longer.
- Never soak woollen items.
- Soak clothes in a bucket or tub large enough so that the items are not tightly bunched.
- Agitate the items by using plumber's plunger or pick the clothes up and drop them back into the water several times. Gently knead with your hands to help remove the dirt.
- Rinse several times in water until there is no hint of detergent left. Add 125 mL of white vinegar to get rid of any soap residue with the final rinse.
- Drip-dry items if possible or roll up in a clean dry towel to remove moisture.

Soaking and bleaching

Items that are heavily soiled will benefit from soaking before adding to the normal wash. Soaking in ordinary washing detergent will normally have the same effect as using a proprietary soaking product. Soaking helps to loosen soiling or dirt so that when the clothes are washed the dirt will be removed more easily.

Bleaching, on the other hand, takes the colour out of dirty marks, making them look as if the marks have gone. Soaking for a short time in bleach will also help loosen the dirt in the same way as soaking in ordinary detergent. Bleaching is really only useful when you want to whiten the whites, add brightness to colours and remove difficult dirty marks.

Before you pre-soak, scrape off any mud, dirt or food debris. Check the care label to see if the fabric can be soaked and then place in a tub or bucket with dissolved detergent and leave overnight or for at least two hours. Rub a little neat detergent on grubby cuffs and collars and on grimy spots, then leave to soak for as long as is necessary or practical. Squeeze as much water as possible out of the items before putting them in the washing machine, or continue to hand wash as directed.

If your washing machine has a pre-soak setting, use this for really soiled items instead of soaking in a bucket or tub. Make sure items soaking are not overcrowded.

If the method of pre-soaking does not remove dirty marks, try using a laundry bleach or check the Stain Removal Guide (pages 112–136).

There are two main types of laundry bleach:

- chlorine bleach with the active ingredient sodium hypochlorite is normally sold in liquid form and is called 'household bleach' or 'all purpose bleach'. It can be used in the laundry as well as for household jobs.
- non-chlorine bleach known as 'colour safe' bleach comes either in liquid form with hydrogen peroxide as the active ingredient, or in powder form with either sodium percarbonate or sodium perborate as the active ingredient. This type of bleach is often sold as a laundry bleach and may have other additives such as water softeners, brighteners and bactericides. This bleach may be used on fabrics where chlorine bleach is not recommended. Check all care labels before proceeding.

Wear rubber gloves when using bleach, always dilute it, be careful not to spill it and always make sure you replace the cap properly. Bleach can damage skin and cause vomiting if swallowed and should be treated with care. Store out of the reach of children and pets.

Bleach may vary in strength depending on the brand and it should be diluted before using. Add approximately 1 part bleach to 10 parts water for a mild solution. Bleach works quite quickly—fifteen minutes may be long enough. Items left for any length of time in bleach may be damaged and weakened. Always thoroughly rinse bleach out of any items before washing.

Care labels should indicate if chlorine bleach can be used. It must *never* be used on silk, wool, leather, nylon, rayon, Elastane, Spandex and drip-dry cottons, or any fabric with a special finish.

Never use bleach with ammonia—poisonous gas is created.

Colour safe bleach should be used only on whites when chlorine beach cannot be used and on coloured items to brighten them. It is more effective to soak them in a warm water solution than cold. It can be safe to use on some silks and wool—read the care label first.

Hydrogen peroxide is a milder bleach and is available through chemists. It can also be used on silks and wool and on delicate fabrics for stain removal. Dilute 1 part hydrogen peroxide with 6 parts water.

Do not use on nylon fabrics or any fabrics with a special finish.

Lemon juice and sunlight are natural bleaches and can certainly be considered as alternatives to chemical bleaches.

Loading the washing machine

How many times have we crammed a large load in the washing machine, hoping for the best? Most washing machines have a maximum load guide. You can weigh the wash in a bag on the bathroom scales or weigh yourself holding the wash and subtract your weight. Depending on the size of the machine, dry weight of clothes for front loaders is around 3–5 kg, for twin tubs about 2.5–3 kg and for top loaders about 3.5–8 kg.

For a better and more efficient wash mix smaller items with larger items and make sure there's enough room for load to agitate properly.

Laundry detergents

Measure the recommended amount of washing detergent for the size of the load. It is possible to use a little less than the recommended quantity and still achieve a good result. Using too much detergent, however, can make items look dull and grey. It can also cause problems for the washing machine with too many suds.

If washing with cold water, it's a good idea to dissolve the washing detergent before adding to the load, although some cold-water detergents do not need dissolving.

Fabric softeners are usually used in the final rinse. They add a conditioning waxlike chemical which adheres to material fibres and gives them a protective coating as well as making them feel soft. They often contain perfume. They reduce the build-up of static electricity and creasing in man-made fibres and can make ironing easier. Towels are an obvious choice as well as sweatshirts and T-shirts. It is a good idea to be a bit discerning when using fabric softeners, which may irritate sensitive skins.

Do not pour fabric conditioner directly on to fabrics as it can cause staining and be difficult to remove. If this happens, rinse the item under cold running water and use a little detergent to remove the stain.

When the wash has finished remove the clothes and wipe out the machine if you are not using it again. Unplug the machine and make sure the rubber door seals are wiped over to remove any moisture; clean out the soap and fabric softener dispensers and the filter regularly. Run the washing machine on a short warm washing cycle with 4–5 litres of distilled white vinegar to clean out any residual soap scum.

Drying

How clothes are dried can save ironing time later. To begin with, never leave wet items in the washing machine or laundry basket for any length of time as colours may run and mildew and a musty smell will develop. The care label should be a guide to the best way of drying items. Wool and certain cotton knits should be dried flat and care should be taken not to pull them out of shape.

Clothes can be dried naturally anywhere there is a flow of air and some sunlight. Use a clothes rack on a balcony or in small garden. Do not overcrowd the rack, make sure there is enough space for air to circulate round the items. A foldaway drying rack or pulley rack can be fixed in the laundry, carport or garage and works well if you get a good through breeze.

Tumble driers are marvellous when the monsoon season has set in but try to line dry most of the time and use the machine only in drying emergencies.

A couple of ways to catch lint in the drier are to soak a face washer in a small bowl of fabric softener, then squeeze out until damp and place in the drier with the damp clothes, or to add half a metre of nylon net to the load.

If you have overdried clothes so they are wrinkled and difficult to iron, put them back in the drier with a damp towel and tumble for 5–8 minutes to dampen the items ready for ironing or hanging.

LINE DRYING

Line drying lets the sun naturally bleach and sterilise towels, sheets, nappies, tea-towels and clothes.

Care labels will indicate if the item can be dried in direct sunlight; some colours and dark materials can fade in strong sunlight and should be dried in the shade.

Peg items out so that when you take them off the line they can be folded and put away without ironing.

Peg trousers, shorts and skirts from the waistband.

Peg T-shirts, shirts and dresses from the bottom hem.

Pleated items should be placed in a stocking and hung up on the line so that the pleats remain crisp.

Sheets dry more quickly if not folded before pegging on the line, but if there is a lack of space, fold them in four and hang, turning them during drying. This can also be done with large tablecloths and towels.

Shirts can be put on plastic hangers to dry on the line; use a rubber band to secure it to the line with a peg.

Flattening, pressing and ironing

If you make a habit of buying easy-care, drip-dry, crease-resistant fabrics you may never have to plug in the iron. Many other items can be taken off the line and folded straightaway or hung directly on clothes hangers and put away. Creases can be pressed by putting the items between the mattress and base of the bed, while unwanted creases can often be removed by hanging the things in the steamy atmosphere of the bathroom.

Leaving items hanging or folded until you're ready to iron rather than leaving them in the ironing basket to get wrinkled also saves work when ironing.

If you have too many clothes squashed together in a wardrobe or jammed into drawers, they will get creased before you wear them. Pack away clothes you do not wear seasonally, and if you haven't worn some things for five years—think about recycling or giving them to charity.

Pressing items   Put a piece of cotton cloth between the item and the iron and gently press—do not glide up and down. Press woollen or knitted items, delicate fabrics, collars and cuffs on jackets or coats.

Ironing items   Adjust the setting for the material you are ironing. Use a steam iron or a spray bottle to add more moisture to help remove creases. Ironing tea towels and handkerchiefs on a very hot setting will sterilise them and this could be an alternative to bleaching.

Spread a tablecloth or sheet out and put on it items that need to be spray starched.

MACHINE DRYING

Give items an extra spin in the washing machine to remove as much moisture as possible before placing in the drier.

Wrap particularly heavy items in a dry towel to remove moisture before putting into the drier.

Follow care label instructions for the correct settings.

Do not overload the drier as it will take longer for everything to dry.

Remove clothing when it is still a little damp and hang on coat-hangers.

Most man-made fibres should be dried on a low heat setting.

Any items with rubber or elastic should not be put in the drier.

Anything with permanent pleats should not be put in the drier—they are normally drip-dry only.

Gently spray over each item before you start to iron. This prevents the spray going all over the floor which becomes slippery, and also stops a build-up of starch on the ironing board.

When the ironing is finished remember to switch off the iron and let it cool before putting it away. If you have to leave the ironing—to answer the phone or the door, always turn it off and make sure it is not resting on anything it can scorch.

IRONING TIPS

Read the instructions to get the best results achievable from your iron.

To clean non-stick plates use a warm cloth and detergent.

To clean an ordinary iron, rub a little bicarbonate of soda over the plate with a damp cloth. Heat the iron to warm and iron over a piece of waxed paper.

Unclog steam vents with a cotton bud and warm soapy water.

Remove starch marks by rubbing over a little warm olive oil.

Metal polish will clean the plate of most ordinary irons.

To restore scratches and to add gloss to an old ironing plate, rub over with dampened salt and crumpled newspaper.

Use distilled water only if the water in your area has a high mineral content. Distilled water keeps the water compartment cleaner.

Never iron over metal objects that may scratch the ironing plate, especially with non-stick plates; use a pressing cloth when necessary to protect the plate.

Be careful not to iron over plastic buttons or zips which may melt onto the plate. If you have, try removing the melted plastic from the plate by ironing a piece of aluminium foil with salt sprinkled over it.

GENERAL RULES FOR IRONING

FABRIC	IRONING HEAT	DAMP OR DRY	WHICH SIDE
Cotton			
pale colours	Hot	Either	Either
dark colours	Hot	Either	Wrong side
Linen			
pale colours	Hot	Either	Either
dark colours	Warm	Damp	Wrong side
Silk	Warm	Dry	Either
	Cool	Damp	Either
Rayon	Warm	Damp	Wrong
Nylon	Cool	Damp	Either
Acrylic	Cool	Dry	Wrong
Polyester	Cool	Damp	Either
Polyester mixes	Warm	Either	Either
Wool fibres	Warm	Dry	Wrong

Chapter 7

SPILLS AND STAINS

There is nothing more annoying than putting on a new outfit and going out to show it off, only to drip the sauce from a dainty canape all down the front of it. Do you sue the host for the dry-cleaning bill or have a go at spot cleaning yourself? Or when friends with small children come to visit and although you have taken every precaution to prevent little hands grabbing the tomato sauce bottle—eh voilà, over it goes, down the padded dinning room chair onto the cat and finally into the pale blue carpet!

You have to ask yourself does it really matter? Will these accidental tragedies make your life a misery from here on in? What you have to remember is that 95 per cent of stains will come out. The material may fade and never look the same if you treat it in a radical way, but even then there are some options to rectify this problem. (Some options are recycling items of clothing, altering them or placing a patch over the mark. You may be able to remake cushion covers to hide the mark, or use a throw rug over the arms, back or even seat of a chair or sofa. Stains on a carpet can be hidden with rugs or by putting furniture over them.)

The method you choose to remove a stain will depend on what the stain is and on the type of material. (See chapter 6, 'Washing and ironing' for a guide to what fabrics are made from.) Although care labelling may tell you not to use bleach or soak items and never use dry-cleaning fluid, sometimes these methods can be used to spot remove stains. Always check to see what material the stained item is made from, if you are not sure, then start off with a mild stain-removing tactic.

THE IMPORTANT FIRST STEPS

Attend to the stain immediately—the longer it stays there the harder it will be to remove.

Use cold water unless otherwise specified—hot water will set the stain and it will be even harder to remove.

Use clean white absorbent materials or pale colourfast material for mopping up stains—old towels, nappies, serviettes or sheets are ideal.

If possible, clean the stain from the reverse side of the fabric first, and from the outside of the stain towards the centre.

Be cautious when applying any stain-removing solvent—test the fabric first in an area that will not be obvious.

Rinse out any solvent thoroughly before trying another method of stain removal.

Try not to soak upholstery or carpets with too much water.

Silk and other expensive materials can be hard to spot clean so take to a reputable drycleaner for expert advice and service.

Never mix solvents together and follow the instructions as directed.

If the stain does not come out immediately, you may need to repeat the process for total success. If the stain is made up of a combination of, say, grease and acid, it may be necessary to use two stain-removal techniques.

If you have a real disaster and the mark will not budge, do not despair—think about recycling or patching. Make the item short-sleeved, remove the collar or cuffs, wear it to paint in, move a chair over the faded spot in the carpet.

WHAT TO HAVE IN YOUR STAIN REPAIR KIT

protective gloves (cotton and rubber)

water spray bottle

large sponge

sea sponge

absorbent white cloths

white paper towels

cotton buds

toothbrush

plastic kitchen scraper

eye dropper

hairdrier

glycerine

petroleum jelly

talcum powder

fullers earth

bicarbonate of soda

salt

borax

proprietary dry-cleaning fluid

chlorine (household) bleach

hydrogen peroxide

cloudy ammonia

white vinegar

lemon juice

soap flakes (pure soap such as Lux)

washing-up detergent

woolwash detergent

enzyme detergent with sodium percarbonate

carpet shampoo

washing soda (sodium carbonate)

non-oily nail-polish remover (acetone)

methylated spirits

white spirit

amyl acetate

soda water

mineral turpentine (turps)

turpentine

eucalyptus oil

tea-tree oil

And don't forget a good supply of water and a clean non-reactive flat surface (a glazed tile or glass plate) as a work surface for chemical applications.

When tackling a stain there are three main methods—absorption, flushing with water, and/or the use of bleach or a solvent.

Absorbents such as talcum powder and fullers earth are used for 'blotting up' liquid or moist greasy spills.

Flushing with cold water first (unless otherwise specified) is to water down and flush the stain out of the material.

Bleaching is used if the stain persists after flushing and using a detergent. Vinegar, cloudy ammonia, lemon juice and an enzyme detergent may be used instead of chlorine bleach or hydrogen peroxide. See bleaching in chapter 6, 'Washing and ironing' for fabric care and use of bleach.

Solvents including borax, turpentine, white spirit and washing soda are used to shift difficult oil or grease stains. Use the absorption method first to remove most of the stain and then carefully apply a solvent to lift out the remainder.

CAUTION

Do not use

- Methylated spirits on rayon or acetate materials

- Non-oily nail-polish remover, undiluted methylated spirits, white spirit, chlorine bleach or too much water when sponging or rinsing on acrylic carpets.

- Chlorine bleach, undiluted cloudy ammonia or too much water when flushing or sponging on wool carpets.

- Oily nail-polish remover, chlorine bleach on nylon.

Before using any of thc following methods always test a small patch of the fabric in an area that will not be noticed before proceeding with bleach, dry-cleaning fluid, grease solvents and other chemicals which could damage the fabric.

Unless otherwise stated apply the spot removal solvent neat.

Where solutions are mentioned in the Stain Removal Guide, use the following proportions if no specific directions are given.

For mild solutions:
chlorine bleach: 1 part to 10 parts water
hydrogen peroxide: 1 part to 8 parts water
borax: 2 tablespoons to 500 mL water
washing soda: 2 heaped tablespoons to 1 litre water
cloudy ammonia (contains soap): 1 part to 3 parts water
white vinegar: 1 part to 3 parts water
bicarbonate of soda: 1 teaspoon to 2 tablespoons water

For strong solutions, increase by 2 parts to the proportion of water shown above.

Use **eucalyptus oil** undiluted unless stated otherwise.

Where **detergent** (washing-up liquid) is mentioned, use a few drops to 1 litre of water.

Woolwash detergents are specifically designed for washing woollen and delicate items. They are normally phosphate-free, biodegradable and very mild. They often contain eucalyptus oil.

Enzyme or biological detergents contain different enzymes that each deal with different stains.

Cross references in the Stain Removal Guide refer to other headings in this section unless otherwise specified.

CAUTION

Many of the products used to remove stains are toxic and must be used with care. Always read the instructions on the label before using them and strictly adhere to any safety precautions. If in doubt, contact the product manufacturer. Store in a safe place, preferably a securely locked cupboard, out of the reach of children.

Stain	Washable	Non-washable	Carpet
ACIDS	Strong acids such as hydrochloric or sulphuric acid can damage fibres, weaker ones like vinegar or acetic acid are not so destructive. Attend to the spill immediately using appropriate safety precautions. Rinse under the cold tap, then apply bicarbonate of soda or a mild mixture of cloudy ammonia and water to neutralise the acid. Rinse and wash as normal.	Blot immediately. Apply bicarbonate of soda, then flush with a mild solution of cloudy ammonia and water. Rinse thoroughly with cold water.	As for non-washable.
ADHESIVE TAPE or STICKY LABELS	Soak the label or tape with warm water, gently peel or rub off. Wash as normal.	Dab with tea-tree oil, then rinse with warm water.	As for non-washable.
ADHESIVES CONTACT GLUE (cellulose-based)	Apply non-oily nail-polish remover or acetone. Dab to remove glue, then rinse and wash as normal. On acetates use amyl acetate.	As for washable.	As for washable and follow up with carpet shampoo.
EPOXY GLUE	Before glue sets, apply methylated spirits, then rinse with water and wash as normal. Once glue sets it is impossible to remove.	As for washable.	As for washable. If glue has set, try trimming the pile carefully with nail scissors, razor blade or electric shaver.

Stain	Washable	Non-washable	Carpet
LATEX GLUE	Before it dries, apply a damp soft sponge to remove any deposits. If dry, apply tea-tree oil, then flush with water and wash as normal.	As for washable. If dry, try removing with a rubber. If difficult to remove, apply a little tea-tree oil and then rinse.	As for non-washable.
PVA GLUE (polyvinyl acetate)	Sponge with methylated spirits or dry-cleaning fluid. Flush with water and wash as normal.	As for washable.	As for washable.
REUSABLE ADHESIVE (Blu-tack)	*see* PLASTICINE		
SUPERGLUE (Cyano-acrylates)	Soak in water until the glue dissolves or can be peeled off, wash as normal.	As for washable.	As for washable. Alternatively, trim away the pile if it will not be noticed.
ALKALIS	Like acids, alkalis such as cloudy ammonia, sodium hydroxide and caustic soda can destroy the fibres of materials so attend to any spill immediately. Rinse immediately with cold water, then flush to neutralise with white vinegar or lemon juice. Wash as normal.	Blot immediately and sponge with white vinegar to neutralise. Rinse thoroughly and dry.	As for non-washable.
ANTI-PERSPIRANT	*see* DEODORANT		

Stain	Washable	Non-washable	Carpet
BALLPOINT PEN	Use a cotton bud to dab the mark with methylated spirits. When ink dissolves, blot and apply more methylated spirits. Rinse and wash as normal.	Dab with methylated spirits until the mark disappears. Rinse thoroughly. Alternatively, take to professional drycleaner.	Apply dry-cleaning fluid to the mark and dab several times, blotting with absorbent paper. Rinse and apply woolwash detergent. Rinse with water, blot dry.
BARBECUE SAUCE	*see* CHUTNEY		
BEER, COCKTAILS, MIXED ALCOHOLIC DRINKS, SOFT DRINKS	Blot and flush with cold water, soak in equal parts white vinegar and warm water for 30 minutes. For stubborn stains apply a paste of enzyme detergent and water. Rinse and then wash as normal.	Blot and sponge with equal parts white vinegar and water. If stain persists try a mild solution of hydrogen peroxide.	Flush with soda water or cold water. Blot up with absorbent materials. Use carpet shampoo, blot and sponge rinse with equal parts white vinegar and water, blot with absorbent material.
BEETROOT JUICE	Flush immediately with cold water. Sponge with a paste of enzyme detergent and cold water, then rinse and wash as normal.	Sponge with cold water immediately to remove as much juice as possible. Keep flushing until no trace left. Sponge rinse with equal parts white vinegar and water.	Sponge with cold water several times to absorb stain. Use equal parts vinegar and cold water to rinse. Sponge on woolwash detergent, rinse with water, then blot.
BIRD DROPPINGS	Scrape off excess and soak in enzyme detergent. Use a mild bleach if stain persists.	Scrape off excess and sponge with a mild cloudy ammonia solution, rinse with white vinegar and then sponge with clean cold water. Blot dry.	As for non-washable.

Stain	Washable	Non-washable	Carpet
BLOOD	Sponge, soak and flush fresh blood stains with cold water immediately. Soak in salty cold water or wash in enzyme detergent. For dried blood, brush off any dry residue. Make a paste with bicarbonate of soda or enzyme detergent and water and gently work over the mark. Leave for 30 minutes then thoroughly rinse. Alternatively, use a mild solution of hydrogen peroxide. Rinse thoroughly and wash as normal.	Sponge with cold water then apply a solution of 1 teaspoon cloudy ammonia to 1 litre of water. Blot and then sponge rinse with cold water.	Flush with cold water or soda water and then blot. Use a woolwash detergent. Try a mild solution of cloudy ammonia and cold water if stain difficult to remove, then rinse and blot dry.
BLUSHER, CREAM POWDERED	*see* LIPSTICK *see* EYESHADOW		
BLU-TACK (reusable adhesive)	*see* PLASTICINE		
BUBBLE GUM	*see* CHEWING GUM		
BUTTER, CHEESE, CHEESE SAUCE	Scrape off any excess and blot. Flush with the hottest water the fabric can stand, blot, then apply a grease solvent such as eucalyptus oil. Wash as normal.	Scrape off any excess, cover with an absorbent powder such as talcum and leave for at least 5 hours. Scrape off, then use a grease solvent. Rinse and blot dry.	As for non-washable. After using the grease solvent such as methylated spirits, sponge with carpet shampoo, rinse then blot dry.

Stain	Washable	Non-washable	Carpet
CANDLE WAX	Gently scrape off immediately, then put an ice cube on the spot or place item in the freezer. When wax is hard, scrape off residue with a spoon. Place several layers of paper towel on each side of the material and press with a hot iron. If colour from the candle remains, apply dry-cleaning fluid. Wash as normal.	As for washable.	As for washable.
CAR POLISH and WAX	Apply dry-cleaning fluid then liquid detergent. Rinse thoroughly then wash as normal.	Dab with dry-cleaning fluid, then thoroughly rinse with water.	As for non-washable.
CARBON PAPER	Dab methylated spirits over the stain. Rinse thoroughly. Alternatively, apply dry-cleaning fluid, then rinse. If stain persists soak in 1 part cloudy ammonia mixed with 3 parts water. Rinse thoroughly and wash as normal. *See also* TONER.	Apply methylated spirits with a cotton bud, blot and apply again until stain is flushed out. Rinse thoroughly.	As for non-washable.
CAROB	*see* CHOCOLATE		
CHEESE, CHEESE SAUCE	*see* BUTTER		

Stain	Washable	Non-washable	Carpet
CHEWING GUM and BUBBLE GUM	If possible place the article in the freezer or put an ice cube or frozen compress over the spot. When gum is hard, crack and peel it off. Spot clean with eucalyptus oil for any residue. Rinse thoroughly and wash as normal.	Apply the ice-cube method, scrape off when hard. Spot clean with eucalyptus oil or methylated spirits.	As for non-washable.
CHOCOLATE, CHOCOLATE SAUCE, COCOA POWDER, COCOA or CHOCOLATE MILK, CAROB	Scrape off any excess, then sponge with a paste made of enzyme detergent and very hot water. Sponge rinse. Wash as normal. For CHOCOLATE MILK *see also* MILK AND MILK PRODUCTS	Use method as for washable, then apply an equal mix of methylated spirits and cloudy ammonia. Blot and rinse thoroughly.	Scrape off excess, sponge with woolwash detergent and rinse with warm water. Use equal amounts of cloudy ammonia and cold water and sponge rinse. Sponge rinse with warm water.
CHUTNEY, TOMATO or BARBECUE SAUCE, PICKLES, MUSTARD	Scrape off any deposits, flush immediately with cold water. Apply a paste of enzyme detergent and water, rinse in cold water and wash as normal.	Scrape off any deposits and sponge with 1 part vinegar, 1 part woolwash detergent and 6 parts water. Blot, sponge rinse with cold water, and blot to dry.	Scrape off any deposits and sponge with vinegar, then with woolwash detergent. Blot and sponge rinse. If the stain persists, try sponging with methylated spirits.
COCOA	*see* CHOCOLATE		
COCKTAILS	*see* BEER		
COFFEE and TEA	Flush stain with cold water, then apply paste of enzyme detergent and water. Rinse and wash as normal.	Sponge with cold water then apply a paste of powdered borax and water. Brush off after 20 minutes and sponge rinse. Alternatively, dry-clean.	Blot immediately and sponge with woolwash detergent and vinegar, then blot. Rinse with cold water and blot. Glycerine may loosen an old stain.

Stain	Washable	Non-washable	Carpet
COLA DRINKS	Flush with cold water, apply neat woolwash detergent, flush with cold water again. Wash as normal. If stain persists, try 1 part methylated spirits, 1 part vinegar and 4 parts cold water. Rinse thoroughly.	Sponge with cold water. Loosen stain with neat glycerine, blot and rinse. Apply 1 part methylated spirits and 2 parts water if stain still obstinate. Rinse thoroughly.	Flush with soda water and blot. Sponge with equal amounts of water and vinegar, and blot.
CRAYON	Gently rub with liquid detergent and rinse until mark is removed. If indelible crayon, use dry-cleaning fluid or methylated spirits.	Use dry-cleaning fluid or take to professional drycleaner.	Apply woolwash detergent to the spot. Rinse with cold water and blot. Apply methylated spirits or dry-cleaning fluid if stain persists.
CREAM and SOUR CREAM	*see* MILK AND MILK PRODUCTS		
CURRY	Scrape off any excess, flush with water, then apply a paste of enzyme detergent and water and leave for 20 minutes. Rinse and wash as normal. Use a weak solution of hydrogen peroxide for any residual staining. Rinse and wash as normal.	Scrape off excess, sponge with an equal solution of cloudy ammonia and water, blot and sponge until stain is removed. If stain persists, apply methylated spirits and sponge and blot. Alternatively, take to a professional drycleaner.	Scrape and blot any excess, apply method for non-washable. If stain persists, sponge with methylated spirits, followed by woolwash detergent, then rinse with a mixture of 1 part vinegar and 2 parts water. Blot dry.
DAIRY DESSERTS	*see* MILK AND MILK PRODUCTS		

Stain	Washable	Non-washable	Carpet
DEODORANT, ANTI-PERSPIRANT	Sponge with a paste of bicarbonate of soda and cold water, leave for several hours. Rinse out. and wash in an enzyme detergent. Alternatively, use dry-cleaning fluid if possible.	Try the above methods or take to the drycleaners.	N/A
EGG	Blot and scrape off excess, flush in cold water, or soak in salty cold water. Wash as normal. If stain persists, sponge with a mild solution of hydrogen peroxide with a few drops of cloudy ammonia added. Rinse and wash as normal.	Blot and scrape off excess, sponge with a mild solution of woolwash detergent. Rinse with cold water and blot.	As for non-washable.
EYESHADOW or BLUSHER, POWDERED	Gently shake, brush or scrape off immediately. Make a paste with enzyme detergent and water and gently rub over the stain. Rinse well. Alternatively, use methylated spirits. Wash as normal.	Use methylated spirits or if stubborn 1 part cloudy ammonia with 3 parts cold water. Rinse.	As for non-washable.
EYESHADOW, CREAM or STICK	see LIPSTICK		

Stain	Washable	Non-washable	Carpet
FAECES	Scrape off any solid mass then flush with cold water. If necessary soak in enzyme detergent or a solution of ½ cup of borax to 10 litres cold water to remove any stubborn stains. Rinse and wash as normal.	Scrape off any solid mass, blot and flush with cold water. Blot with a mild solution of cloudy ammonia and water. Rinse with cold water.	Apply the same method as non-washable. Use mild woolwash detergent to sponge clean, then rinse and blot dry.
FAT	*see* GRAVY AND SAUCE		
FELT-TIP PEN	Difficult to remove unless dealt with immediately. Dab with methylated spirits or apply a paste of enzyme detergent and water to the spot and gently rub. Wash as normal.	Apply methylated spirits to the spot or take to professional drycleaner.	Apply dry-cleaning fluid, blot, then apply carpet shampoo. Rinse with clean water and blot again.
FISH	Flush with a solution of 20mL cloudy ammonia, 20 mL detergent and 1 litre warm water. Rinse in cold water. Apply a paste of enzyme detergent and water. Rinse thoroughly. Wash as normal.	Sponge several times with cold water. Sponge with a mild cloudy ammonia solution and blot. Rinse with cold water and blot.	As for non-washable.
FOUNDATION CREAM or LIQUID	Scrape off excess. Cover with talcum powder and leave to absorb grease, then scrape off. Soak in 10 mL cloudy ammonia mixed in 1 litre of water. Wash normally. Alternatively, use dry-cleaning fluid, then wash.	Blot up or scrape off excess. Use dry-cleaning fluid or try methylated spirits.	As for non-washable.

Stain	Washable	Non-washable	Carpet
FROMAGE FRAIS	*see* MILK AND MILK PRODUCTS		
FRUIT and VEGETABLE JUICES (berries, fruit juice drinks)	Flush immediately with cold water until the water runs clear. If stain persists and the fabric allows, stretch the fabric with the stained area over a saucepan and pour boiling water onto the stain from 90 cm above. Use a mild solution of hydrogen peroxide if necessary. Wash as normal.	Sponge with cold water and blot until stain disappears. Apply glycerine if stain persists and leave for two hours then sponge rinse with cold water. Alternatively, try dry-cleaning fluid or take to the drycleaner.	Blot immediately, sponge with cold water and blot until the stain disappears. Sponge with woolwash detergent, rinse and blot. Apply methylated spirits to the spot if difficult to remove
FURNITURE POLISH	Blot the stain and apply a dry-cleaning solvent, rinse and wash as normal.	Blot and apply a dry-cleaning solvent, or take to professional drycleaner.	Blot with absorbent paper, and then try dry-cleaning solvent. Rinse and apply carpet shampoo.
GRASS	Apply methylated spirits or dry-cleaning fluid. Rinse thoroughly and wash as normal. To loosen old stains rub in neat glycerine and leave for about 1 hour. Follow with methylated spirits, then flush with water. Wash as normal.	Sponge with methylated spirits or eucalyptus oil, then thoroughly rinse. Repeat several times. Alternatively, take to a drycleaner.	N/A

Stain	Washable	Non-washable	Carpet
GRAVY and SAUCE (fat, stock, colouring, salad dressing, mayonnaise, thickening agents, cooked meat juice)	Scrape off excess, then sponge with cold water. Use a grease solvent. Rinse then wash as normal.	Scrape off excess, then sponge with dry-cleaning fluid. Alternatively, take to professional drycleaner.	Scrape off excess, apply dry-cleaning fluid. Rinse then apply carpet shampoo.
GREASE	*see* OIL		
HAIR DYE (treat chemically based and vegetable dyes such as henna the same)	To stop dye running, spray with hair spray, then flush with cold water. Apply a paste of enzyme detergent and cold water. Rinse. Use a mild solution of hydrogen peroxide on any residual colour. Rinse and wash.	Blot and then take to a professional drycleaner.	Use dry-cleaning fluid, followed by carpet shampoo.
HAIR SPRAY	Flush with water, soak in enzyme detergent, rinse well.	Sponge with methylated spirits or dry-cleaning fluid.	Use carpet shampoo and vacuum when dry.
HONEY	*see* JAM		
ICE CREAM	*see* MILK AND MILK PRODUCTS		
INK, FOUNTAIN PEN	Blot immediately, then flush with cold water until the stain disappears. Apply equal parts of water and cloudy ammonia, then rinse. Wash as normal. *See also* BALLPOINT PEN	Blot the stain immediately, dab with methylated spirits and then blot. Alternatively, take to the drycleaner.	As for washable.

Stain	Washable	Non-washable	Carpet
IODINE	Attend to immediately as it will stain most fabrics brown. Flush with water then apply a paste of enzyme detergent and water. Leave on for a while then rinse. Wash as normal. Alternatively, soak the spot with clean water and leave out in direct sunlight or steam over a kettle. Use a mild bleach solution if the stain persists.	Blot then flush with white spirit several times and rinse. Alternatively, try methylated spirits, then thoroughly rinse.	Blot up any excess, then dab with methylated spirits. Rinse then sponge with woolwash detergent and rinse.
IRON MOULD or RUST	see RUST		
JAM, MARMALADE, HONEY	Scrape off any excess, flush with warm water and then apply a paste of enzyme detergent and water. Rinse thoroughly. Wash as normal. Use a mild bleach solution if stain persists.	Scrape off any excess, flush with warm water. Mix a paste of a little borax, detergent and water and place over the stain. Leave for several minutes. Rinse thoroughly.	Scrape off any excess, sponge with warm water. Sponge with woolwash detergent, rinse and blot.
LACQUER	see VARNISH AND LACQUER		
LIPSTICK, LIPLINER, CREAM or STICK EYESHADOW or BLUSHER	Blot up or scrape off any excess, gently rub with glycerine or petroleum jelly to loosen it. If reluctant, try methylated spirits or grease solvent such as white spirit or dry-cleaning fluid. Wash as normal.	Use a dry-cleaning fluid but if no success take to a professional drycleaner.	Use dry-cleaning fluid, followed by woolwash detergent, then flush with water, blot with a towel and use a hairdryer if necessary to dry.

Stain	Washable	Non-washable	Carpet
MASCARA	Make a paste with enzyme detergent and water and gently rub out the mark, rinse and wash as normal. Use dry-cleaning solvent if mark is hard to shift.	Sponge with methylated spirits or 1 part cloudy ammonia with 3 parts cold water. Rinse.	As for non-washable.
MAYONNAISE	see GRAVY and SAUCE		
MEAT and MEAT JUICES, UNCOOKED COOKED	see BLOOD see GRAVY and SAUCE		
MEDICINE, LIQUID	Liquid medicines may be carried in a sugar syrup, oil, tar, alcohol or iron base. You may need to check to see what is in the medicine and treat the stain appropriately. Iron-based medicine stains, for example, should be treated as for iron mould or rust stains. Use this treatment for most sugar syrup medicines.		
	Flush with cold water and then apply a paste of enzyme detergent and water. Rinse thoroughly and wash as normal.	Flush with warm water, apply a mixture of 2 tablespoons of borax to 1 litre of water and detergent to the spot. Sponge the area then rinse thoroughly. Use methylated spirits, where applicable, to remove any colour stain.	Sponge with warm water, apply woolwash detergent and sponge the area, rinse then blot.
METAL POLISH	Blot immediately to remove any excess, then flush with cold water. Blot dry and apply methylated spirits. Rinse well and wash as normal.	Blot immediately, then flush repeatedly with dry-cleaning fluid, blotting each time until stain dissolves. If stain persists, take to professional drycleaner.	Blot immediately and then apply dry-cleaning fluid and blot. Apply woolwash detergent, then rinse and blot.

Stain	Washable	Non-washable	Carpet
MILDEW	Brush off with a toothbrush, then apply a paste of enzyme detergent and water. Leave for 30 minutes then rinse and wash as normal. If stain persists, try a mild bleach solution.	Brush off, then apply dry-cleaning fluid or tea-tree oil. Rinse thoroughly.	As for non-washable, then apply carpet shampoo.
MILK and MILK PRODUCTS (cream, fromage frais, ice cream, sour cream, yoghurt)	Scrape off excess, blot immediately then flush with cold water. Soak in enzyme detergent, rinse and wash as normal. When dry, sponge any remaining greasy marks with methylated spirits. Rinse thoroughly. *See also* CHOCOLATE (CHOCOLATE MILK)	Scrape off excess, apply dry-cleaning fluid, then dab with equal parts cold water and methylated spirits. Rinse with cold water.	Scrape off excess, sponge with woolwash detergent and vinegar. Sponge rinse and blot.
MOISTUR-ISER, FACE and BODY CREAM	Scrape up as much residue as possible. Cover with talcum powder and leave to absorb grease, then scrape off. Soak in 10 mL cloudy ammonia mixed in 1 litre of water, then wash in the normal way. If very greasy use methylated spirits or dry-cleaning fluid. Alternatively, use a dry-cleaning fluid, then wash.	Blot up or scrape off excess. Use dry-cleaning fluid or methylated spirits.	As for non-washable.

Stain	Washable	Non-washable	Carpet
MUCUS	Soak in a solution of salt and cold water or mild solution of cloudy ammonia and water. Wash as normal.	Sponge soak with a mild solution of cloudy ammonia and water. Rinse thoroughly.	Sponge with cold water, blot, then sponge with a mild solution of cloudy ammonia and water. Blot and sponge rinse.
MUD	Allow to dry then gently brush off the excess. Any remaining mark can be removed by pre-soaking before washing in the normal way.	Allow to dry and then brush or vacuum off. Sponge remaining mark with liquid detergent, or, if necessary, apply dry-cleaning fluid.	Allow to dry, brush with a stiff brush then vacuum. Apply a carpet shampoo if a stain remains.
MUSTARD	see CHUTNEY		
NAIL POLISH	If a fresh spill, blot up as much up as possible. From the wrong side, dab with non-oily nail-polish remover and carefully flush with white spirit. Use methylated spirits to remove any colour deposits. Do not use this method on rayon or synthetic fabrics, use amyl acetate as a remover (available from chemists). Wash as normal.	Blot up any excess, then use nail-polish remover (if material is not synthetic) or amyl acetate (if a synthetic mix).	As for non-washable. Use dry-cleaning fluid if stain is stubborn.
NEWSPRINT	Apply glycerine to the spot, then rinse and apply a paste of enzyme detergent and water. Wash as normal.	Apply glycerine, then rinse with cloudy ammonia and water solution. Rinse thoroughly.	As for non-washable.

Stain	Washable	Non-washable	Carpet
OIL and GREASE (vegetable and mineral)	Blot immediately with absorbent material to remove any excess. Apply a paste of enzyme detergent and warm water. Rinse and wash as normal. Alternatively, use several applications of a grease solvent, blotting as you apply them. Rinse and wash normally.	Blot any excess, then try methylated spirits or other grease solvent, or take to professional drycleaner.	As for non-washable. Sprinkle liberally with absorbent powder and leave for 3 hours. Vacuum. Apply methylated spirits or dry-cleaning fluid. Sponge rinse with cold water.
PAINT ACRYLIC PAINT (water-based)	Scrape off any excess and blot immediately and then sponge with cold water several times until the stain has disappeared. Wash as normal. Any dried stains can be loosened with methylated spirits and then rinsed before washing as normal. Any difficult residue can be treated with dry-cleaning fluid. Rinse and wash as normal.	Blot and scrape off any excess, dampen with a wet sponge and then sponge with methylated spirits until stain disappears. Alternatively, take to a specialist drycleaner.	Scrape off any excess and blot several times. Apply carpet shampoo and warm water, gently sponge and blot. Try methylated spirits to remove any residual stain. Rinse and then shampoo again.
EMULSION (gloss, matt or flat, water-based)	Scrape off excess and flush with cold water until stain has gone. Soak in detergent and add 2 tablespoons of cloudy ammonia. Wash in the normal way.	Blot excess, dampen with warm water and blot and sponge until stain is diluted. Try methylated spirits mixed with water or dry-cleaning fluid. Alternatively take immediately to a drycleaner.	Blot up excess and sponge rinse with cold water several times. Sponge rinse with a mild cloudy ammonia solution and then apply carpet shampoo.

Stain	Washable	Non-washable	Carpet
OIL PAINT (gloss, matt, flat)	Blot up any excess then dab with turpentine or white spirit until the stain disappears. Repeat several times and then wash as normal in warm water. For rayon or acetate take to a drycleaner.	Blot up excess and then apply turpentine or white spirit and dab until stain disappears. Rinse and then if necessary take to drycleaners.	Blot excess and dab with white spirit or turpentine. Follow with carpet shampoo.
CELLULOSE (craft and hobby oil-based paint)	Blot immediately and spot apply proprietary cellulose thinner (see paint tin), blot and then rinse and wash as normal. Do not use this method on rayon use non-washable method.	Blot immediately and apply dry-cleaning fluid, blot several times. Alternatively, take to a professional drycleaner.	Blot and apply a dry-cleaning solvent. Rinse and apply carpet shampoo.
PARAFFIN	Blot up excess and cover with talcum powder or fullers earth. Leave to absorb for at least 2–3 hours if possible. Scrape off and then apply dry-cleaning fluid. Wash on the hottest setting the fabric can take.	Blot immediately and then apply talcum powder or fullers earth. Scrape off and apply dry-cleaning fluid and flush through. Try lightly pressing the mark with a warm iron between absorbent paper. Alternatively, take to a professional drycleaner.	As for non-washable then apply carpet shampoo.
PENCIL	Try using an eraser, or sponge with liquid detergent and rinse thoroughly. Wash as normal. Alternatively, try dry-cleaning fluid, rinse and wash as normal.	Gently use an eraser, or sponge with dry-cleaning fluid if necessary. Rinse with water.	As for non-washable.

Stain	Washable	Non-washable	Carpet
PERFUME	Flush out immediately with cold water then soak in 1 part cloudy ammonia and 5 parts warm water. For dried stains, gently rub in equal parts glycerine and warm water. Wash as normal.	Sponge on the glycerine and warm water solution as for washable and leave for 30 minutes. Sponge out with warm water. Delicate fabrics may have to be dry-cleaned.	As for non-washable. Follow with a carpet shampoo, vacuum when dry.
PERSPIRA-TION	Sponge with a mild cloudy ammonia and cold water solution and leave. If stain persists, sponge with water and enzyme detergent paste. Rinse thoroughly.	Dab with 1 part white vinegar to 4 parts water. Blot and rinse with cold water. Dry-clean only if acetate or rayon, especially on the lining of a jacket.	N/A
PETROLEUM JELLY	see OIL		
PICKLES	see CHUTNEY		
PLASTICINE, PLAY DOUGH or REUSABLE ADHESIVE	Scrape off excess, apply a paste of enzyme detergent and water and leave for 10 minutes. Rinse and wash as normal.	Scrape off excess, dab several times with a mild solution of cloudy ammonia and water, rinse thoroughly. Alternatively, try a dry-cleaning fluid.	Scrape off excess and dab several times with a mild solution of cloudy ammonia and water, then rinse. Apply a carpet shampoo as directed.
PLAY DOUGH	see PLASTICINE		
PUTTY	Scrape off excess and place in the freezer or apply ice block or frozen compress. Peel off hardened residue, then apply dry-cleaning fluid. Wash on hottest setting the material can take.	As for washable then apply dry-cleaning fluid.	Scrape off excess and apply frozen compress to set the residue. Peel off and apply dry-cleaning fluid. Follow with carpet shampoo.

Stain	Washable	Non-washable	Carpet
REUSABLE ADHESIVE (Blu-tack)	*see* PLASTICINE		
RUST	Dab a paste of lemon juice and salt onto the stain. Leave for about one hour then rinse with cold water. Repeat if stubborn. Alternatively, apply a proprietary rust remover obtainable from the chemist. As this is a strong acid (oxalic acid), it is advisable only to use it on white or very pale colour-fast articles.	Take to professional drycleaner.	Apply a paste of lemon and salt and gently dab into the mark. If difficult to shift apply a proprietary rust remover.
SALAD DRESSING	*see* GRAVY and SAUCE		
SCORCH MARKS	Apply a solution of 3 tablespoons of borax with 500 mL of water. Soak the area until the mark fades. Wash as normal. If difficult to remove from light-coloured article, soak in a mild bleach solution.	Soften the mark with glycerine mixed equally with water and leave for about 1 hour. Rinse with a mild solution of borax and water, then blot.	As for non-washable. If unsuccessful, snip away the burnt fibres, then brush the pile. If a pale-coloured carpet, a mild bleach solution may be applied and then rinsed thoroughly. It may be necessary to patch if the mark is large.
SELF-TANNING LOTION	Soak the stained item in a mild bleach solution, then wash as normal.	Try dry-cleaning fluid or take to professional drycleaner.	Use dry-cleaning fluid followed by carpet shampoo.

Stain	Washable	Non-washable	Carpet
SEMEN	Apply a solution of 1 part cloudy ammonia to 3 parts water and let soak for about 30 minutes. Soak the area with a paste of enzyme detergent and cold water. Use hydrogen peroxide solution if stain persists. Rinse thoroughly and wash normally.	Sponge with cold water then sponge soak with a mild solution of cloudy ammonia and water. Blot and rinse well with cold water.	As for non-washable. Sponge with woolwash detergent, blot, then sponge rinse with cold water.
SHOE POLISH	Scrape off excess, then apply a solution of equal parts of water and cloudy ammonia. Rinse thoroughly, then wash as normal. If stubborn stain, apply white spirit to the spot. Rinse and wash as normal.	Scrape off excess and carefully dab with white spirit. Rinse with water. Alternatively, take to a professional drycleaner.	As for non-washable, then apply a woolwash detergent and then rinse thoroughly.
SOFT DRINK	*see* BEER		
SOOT	Do not brush or rub or you will spread the mark. Lift any loose powder with adhesive tape, then soak spot with tea-tree oil and wash as normal.	Do not brush. Use adhesive tape to lift off any excess or vacuum off as much as possible, cover with talcum powder or fullers earth, leave to absorb, then vacuum again. Use a mild cloudy ammonia solution to rinse and then rinse with water and dry. Alternatively, use a dry-cleaning fluid.	As for non-washable.

Stain	Washable	Non-washable	Carpet
SOUP	Scrape off excess, sponge with a paste of enzyme detergent and water. Rinse thoroughly. Wash as normal.	Scrape off excess, sponge with cold water. Apply methylated spirits and rinse thoroughly. Alternatively, take to a professional drycleaner.	Scrape off excess. Sponge rinse with cold water. Rinse with a mild solution of cloudy ammonia and water. Rinse and blot.
SOUR CREAM	see MILK and MILK PRODUCTS		
STOCK	see GRAVY and SAUCE		
SUGAR SYRUP	see SWEETS		
SUNSCREEN LOTION or CREAM	Apply a paste of enzyme detergent and water and gently rub over the spot. Rinse well. If stain persists try methylated spirits and rinse well, or try a mild solution of hydrogen peroxide. Rinse and wash as normal.	Apply methylated spirits and blot over the stain, leave for a while and blot again. For stubborn stains, try a mild solution of hydrogen peroxide.	As for non-washable.
SWEETS, CARAMELISED SUGAR, TOFFEE, SUGAR SYRUP	Scrape off excess, soak in equal parts of warm water and white vinegar with detergent. Rinse and wash as normal.	Scrape off excess, sponge with a paste of enzyme detergent and water. Rinse with warm water and blot. Spot clean with dry-cleaning fluid if necessary. Rinse with water.	Scrape off excess, sponge with warm water and woolwash detergent, rinse with equal parts of water and vinegar. Blot to absorb moisture.
TAR	Scrape off any excess, soften with glycerine, then apply eucalyptus oil and gently dab to remove. Alternatively, apply dry-cleaning fluid. Rinse and wash on hottest setting material can stand.	Apply glycerine to loosen the stain then apply dry-cleaning fluid and blot several times. If stain persists, take to a professional drycleaner.	Apply glycerine to loosen the mark then apply eucalyptus oil and dab the stain to remove it. Apply carpet shampoo afterwards.

Stain	Washable	Non-washable	Carpet
TEA	*see* COFFEE and TEA		
TOFFEE	*see* SWEETS		
TOMATO SAUCE	*see* CHUTNEY		
TURMERIC	*see* CURRY; HAIR DYE		
TYPEWRITER CORRECTION FLUID	Check whether or not the fluid is water soluble before attempting to remove the stain. If water soluble, treat as for foundation stain, otherwise immediately dab eucalyptus oil or amyl acetate on to the spot, or try correction fluid thinner. Flush and then wash as normal.	As for washable or take to a professional drycleaner.	As for washable, finish with carpet shampoo.
URINE	Flush several times with cold water. Rinse through with white vinegar or a weak solution of cloudy ammonia. Wash as normal. If stain persists, soak in enzyme detergent or apply mild solution of hydrogen peroxide. Rinse and wash as normal.	Sponge soak with equal parts white vinegar or cloudy ammonia and water. Blot and thoroughly rinse with water.	For fresh urine, blot then rinse with equal parts cloudy ammonia with water, blot rinse with white vinegar. Sponge with woolwash detergent, blot, then sponge rinse with cold water.
VARNISH and LACQUER	Blot immediately, then apply methylated spirits. Wash as normal afterwards.	Blot immediately, then flush with methylated spirits or dry-cleaning fluid.	Blot immediately and then flush with dry-cleaning fluid. Follow with carpet shampoo.

Stain	Washable	Non-washable	Carpet
VOMIT	Scrape off excess, blot then flush with cold water. Soak in enzyme detergent. Rinse well. Wash normally.	Scrape off excess then blot. Sponge with a mild solution of cloudy ammonia and water. Rinse thoroughly with cold water.	Scrape off excess and blot. Cover with bicarbonate of soda, then scrape again. Sponge with woolwash detergent. Blot, then sponge rinse with cold water.
WINE, RED	Rinse immediately under cold water or cover with salt, then flush with cold water. Apply a paste of borax and water or enzyme detergent and water and leave for several minutes. Rinse thoroughly. Wash as normal. Alternatively, rinse the stain immediately with white wine or vinegar, or cover the stain with salt and leave for several hours. Wash as normal. Loosen an old stain by applying glycerine, rinse, then sponge with a paste of enzyme detergent and water. Rinse and wash as normal.	Sponge immediately with cold water and blot. Sprinkle liberally with talcum powder or fullers earth and leave for about 30 minutes. Brush off and repeat until the wine is absorbed. Alternatively, take to the drycleaner. Try loosening an old stain with neat glycerine, then sponge with warm water. Gently rub with neat liquid detergent then blot and rinse several times with cold water.	Pour soda water immediately onto the spot and then blot with towels; try several splashes; blotting after each one. If necessary, use carpet shampoo as directed.

Stain	Washable	Non-washable	Carpet
WINE, WHITE (including champagne)	Rinse immediately with cold water and sponge with 3 tablespoons of borax mixed with 500 mL warm water. Alternatively, sponge a paste of cold water and enzyme detergent over the stain. Rinse and wash as normal. Try glycerine sponged over any stubborn, dried wine stains to loosen them. Wash as normal.	As for red wine.	As for red wine.
YOGHURT	*see* MILK and MILK PRODUCTS		

Chapter 8

HOUSEHOLD CLEANING PRODUCTS

Everyday cleaning products that we take for granted abound on our supermarket shelves. It can certainly be challenging to work out just what is the wonder ingredient in the product that will lift off the baked-on grunge from the stove and whether you'll need a full diving outfit to protect your skin and cope with the fumes.

Unfortunately not all product labels are helpful in giving a listing of the various chemical ingredients or detailed information about the possible hazards of their use.

Before buying and then using any household cleaning product carefully read the directions for use and also any caution or warning on the label. Children are the most at risk from getting hold of any of these products and possibly drinking, eating or spilling them on their skin. It is imperative that all household cleaning products are in a safe place where inquisitive hands cannot get hold of them. If you have sensitive skin *always* wear protective gloves and clothing. If you suffer from any respiratory problems, only use cleaning products in a well-ventilated area, or consider using a product that is well diluted or a less harmful cleaner.

The following is a list of commonly used products in the home and their features. A useful, detailed reference book on the chemicals in household products is CHOICE Books' *A-Z of Chemicals in the Home*.

Cross references refer to other headings in this chapter unless otherwise specified.

ACETIC ACID *see* VINEGAR

ACETONE

Used as a solvent to remove nail polish and animal and vegetable oils. It is normally bought in the form of non-oily nail-polish remover or as a paint or varnish stripper. It will dissolve acetate fabrics and it is highly flammable. Always use in a well-ventilated area and away from any naked flame. An alternative is to use lemon juice for stain removal.

AIR FRESHENERS

Normally available in aerosol and in block form. They contain solvents and perfumes and may contain hydrocarbons as propellants. If you have a well-ventilated home these should not be necessary to use. If you leave a bowl containing a few drops of household ammonia, a table-spoon of bicarbonate of soda, a few drops of lavender oil and hot water in a room overnight it will remove any cigarette or cooking smells.

Try lighting a match after using the toilet to remove odours. Alternatively use aromatherapy oils and a burner, or make up your own spray with a mixture of oils, alcohol and water.

AMMONIA

A strong alkaline cleaner which is a mild bleach and a grease solvent. I prefer to use cloudy ammonia which has added soap and contains about 10 per cent household ammonia. Never mix ammonia with other cleaning products. Dilute full strength ammonia with water, 10 per cent only in a solution. Wear protective gloves and make sure the area you are cleaning in is well ventilated.

AMYL ACETATE

Where acetone cannot be used on acetate fabrics as a stain remover, amyl acetate can be effective. Sometimes difficult to obtain these days, but it can be ordered through the chemist and it is sometimes used as a chemical ingredient in some nail-polish removers.

AUTOMATIC DISHWASHING MACHINE DETERGENT

These are usually heavily composed of phosphates and silicates and because of their alkalinity they can corrode glassware, aluminium and glazes on china, and harm some plastics. Some products also may contain chlorine bleach to aid the removal of stains and act as a disinfectant. There are brands available which are phosphate-free and contain no chlorine that are worth using as an alternative. Scrape off or rinse very soiled dishes, always run a full machine and try to use less detergent.

BATHROOM AND KITCHEN CLEANERS

Mostly these are a thick liquid, paste or powder which will contain bleach, abrasives and detergents. Kitchen cleaners normally will be more alkaline and bathroom cleaners will have more acidic compounds. As well as abrasive-type cleaners there are all-purpose cleaners which are also used in the kitchen and bathroom. These contain detergents, ammonia or solvents and sometimes a mild abrasive.

All-purpose bathroom spray cleaners will help to keep mould at bay and dissolve built-up soap scum, but they may contain phosphates, anti-bacterial bleaches, detergents, and perfumes. Use products that will cause the least harm to the environment.

BICARBONATE OF SODA (SODIUM BICARBONATE)

This is sold in a powder form and is a mild alkali. It can be used for a variety of household cleaning purposes, like stain removal from tiles, glass, oven doors, glass and china; cleaning out refrigerators; and helping to remove smells. It acts as a stain remover for fruit juices and mild acids.

BLEACH

This is used to remove colour, stains, mould and also to disinfect household items. It is sold in varying strengths depending on what the job is. The two main types of laundry and household bleach are oxygen and chlorine bleach. Another much milder bleach is hydrogen peroxide which is normally sold through chemists and is used as an alternative for stain removal and mild bleaching and sterilising. Lemon juice is also a bleach and it is safe to use and will often perform just as well as a commercial bleach products. As there are less harmful and less unpleasant ways of cleaning than using bleach, consider them before using what I call the 'last resort' product. Use the sun to sterilise and bleach nappies. There are many air-borne bacteria so that disinfecting surfaces with bleach is really not worth the bother. An alternative way to sterilise household items is to use boiling water and/or dry things in a hot oven; or wipe over the surface with a mild diluted solution of tea-tree oil, followed with a rinse of clean water.

BLUE

This will give a blue tinge to white clothes to make them appear brighter. It is often an additive in laundry detergents so not really worth using unless you have a lot of whites and feel by dying them 'blue' they look better!

BORAX (SODIUM TETRABORATE)

Used as a water softener, disinfectant and stain remover, as well as being an effective ant repellent when mixed with sugar. Sold in powder form or colourless crystalline salt, it is an excellent additive to many household cleaning jobs. It can be bought at the supermarket, hardware stores and the chemist.

CARBOLIC ACID *see* PHENOL

CARPET CLEANERS

Usually sold as a liquid, powder or foaming aerosol product. They will contain detergents and solvents. Powder cleaners are best if you do not want to 'wet' the carpet.

CAUSTIC SODA (SODIUM HYDROXIDE)

A very strong and corrosive alkali often used in drain and oven cleaners. There are other less drastic cleaners than caustic soda which will do the job just as efficiently.

CITRUS-BASED CLEANERS/SOLVENTS

These are a fairly recent addition to the cleaning arsenal. Available in spray bottles, they are pleasant-smelling, have no vapours and are effective in the removal of oils, grease, soap scum and light waxes from a variety of surfaces, including glass, tiles, clothing and even children's hair (for gum removal). These are a great alternative for those concerned about using harsh chemicals around the home.

DESCALING PRODUCTS

These are used to remove mineral deposits or stains from appliances, sinks, baths and bathroom accessories. They contain ammonia and other caustic abrasives. Use other less corrosive products like vinegar, borax or household ammonia.

DETERGENT

Normally refers to synthetic-based cleaners which have in many products replaced soap-based cleaners that were made from animal or vegetable fats. Synthetic detergents will dissolve in hot or cold water, whereas soap-based products do not dissolve in cold water. Soaps will leave a film whereas synthetic detergents do not. Synthetic-based detergents are made from petroleum by-products and may contain different additives depending on the job they are intended to do.

Laundry detergent These detergents can be a combination of synthetic detergent, brighteners, moisturisers, bleach solvents, zeloites, perfumes, phosphates, metal protectors and enzymes. Laundry detergents that contain enzymes assist in breaking down biologically based stains like blood, grass and sweat, and also stains that contain protein and starch. All these additives vary in strength, and for sensitive skins this may cause some irritation.

While phosphates help to 'soften' the water and keep extracted dirt suspended in it, it's best to choose detergents that are phosphate-free. Too much phosphorus in our waterways can cause excessive growth of blue-green algae, which is detrimental to the environment. Use less detergent if possible and buy concentrated detergents as they use less packaging.

Laundry detergent formulated for hand washing is often milder than some of the liquid or powder detergents.

Washing-up detergent A synthetic-based cleaner which may contain degreasers, phosphates, perfume and enzymes. These detergents are much milder than other detergents. Select ones that are biodegradable and phosphate-free with low or no perfume. Washing-up detergent can be used for other household cleaning jobs, and where mild detergent is mentioned in this book, this is the type of detergent referred to. Always wash dishes in hot water and rinse with clean, hot water afterwards. Where possible, recycle grey water onto the garden.

DISHWASHING MACHINE DETERGENT *see* AUTOMATIC DISHWASHING MACHINE DETERGENT

DISINFECTANT

A variety of disinfectant products are used to kill bacteria and germs on surfaces, dishes and on household fabrics. The ingredients found in disinfectants may include chlorine bleach, hydrogen peroxide, phenol, chloroxylenol, quaternary ammonium compounds and triethylene glycol. Using disinfectants can make you feel that your home is 'germ safe', but as most bacteria are air-borne and most disinfectants can cause problems in waterways by killing helpful bacteria (especially in septic tanks), a safer alternative should be used. Try vinegar, lemon juice or tea-tree or eucalyptus oil. Any disinfectant should be used in a diluted form and care should be used not to mix toilet disinfectants with other cleaning products.

DRAIN CLEANERS

Try and avoid blocked drains by not putting things down the drain that should go in the garbage bin or into the compost. Always use sink strainers on the plug-holes to collect food scraps in the kitchen and stray hairs in the bathroom. Drain cleaners can contain toxic and corrosive ingredients causing skin and respiratory problems. Use a sink filled with hot water and washing soda to flush out any blockage, and remember to keep grease, oil, tea-leaves and coffee grounds out of the drain!

DRY-CLEANING FLUID

Sold mainly for spot dry-cleaning, these products are toxic and can cause skin and respiratory problems. Some of them are flammable and care should always be used when spot cleaning anything. The solvent will remove grease and oil when water cannot be used. Sometimes white vinegar or lemon juice might work on some stains. If the fabric is washable try washing first.

EUCALYPTUS OIL

The oil extracted from eucalyptus leaves is a disinfectant and an insecticide. It is often used in household disinfectant products and in woolwash detergent solutions. Used in correct proportions it is a natural and effective disinfectant and stain remover.

FABRIC CONDITIONERS AND SOFTENERS

These are added to the rinse cycle in the laundry to help reduce static in synthetic fabrics. They contain perfumes and waxy lubricants that coat the fibres of materials to make them feel soft to touch. They are not a necessary additive to your wash.

FRENCH CHALK

A fine powdery chalk which is used to absorb grease and oil spills on fabrics.

FULLERS EARTH

A clay mineral powder which is used to absorb oil and grease from non-washable fabrics.

FURNITURE AND FLOOR POLISHES

Most polishes contain waxes or oils as well as perfumes and solvents. Most modern furniture does not require polishing as it is varnished or sealed. Some wooden floors will need to be polished once or twice a year and perhaps more often in heavy traffic areas. Making your own furniture and floor polish is easy and inexpensive, and you will know exactly what is in such polish (see chapter 9, Recipes for Homemade Cleaning Products).

GLYCERINE

A glutinous liquid which is a by-product of fat or oil in soap making, glycerine is used to help soften stubborn stains.

LAUNDRY AIDS

Nappy treatments These treatments are used to soak soiled nappies or other household fabrics (bed linen and tablecloths, tea-towels, face washers) and sterilise and whiten or colour brighten them. The most common chemical ingredient used is sodium perborate along with water softeners and detergent. Alternatives to using nappy treatments include pre-soaking in laundry detergent to loosen any stains, and washing in very hot water (65 °C) or hanging in strong sunlight to kill bacteria.

Pre-wash cleaners These can be bars of soap-like solvents or spray-on cleaners, which contain a variety of chemical ingredients such as solvents, sodium percarbonate, hydrogen peroxide, 'hard' surfactants, perfumes and water softeners. Use soap-based pre-wash products or soak in ordinary laundry detergent before washing where possible.

LINSEED OIL

Raw linseed oil is made from flax seeds and it has virtually no taste or smell. It is used as a furniture oil and to remove stains from wood. Boiled linseed oil is also available. It is highly flammable and toxic, is darker in colour and may be used for a variety of household tasks.

METAL CLEANERS

There's a cleaner for every metal found in the home and some products boast they will clean all metals. Brass and copper cleaners contain abrasives such as pumice or rottenstone, as well as solvents, ammonia, kerosene, or white spirit. Other polishes, especially silver polish, use more acidic chemicals and it is vital that all of the polish is wiped or rinsed off thoroughly to prevent the metal being damaged.

METHYLATED SPIRITS (DENATURED SPIRITS)

This is basically ethanol (pure alcohol) to which additives have been added to make it poisonous. It is highly flammable and may cause skin and respiratory problems. It also will pollute the waterways so do not dispose of it down the sink. It is, however, a household cleaner which can be a stain remover, glass and window cleaner and also used in conjunction with other cleaners. It will polish chrome, jewellery and ivory.

MILDEW AND MOULD CLEANERS

These are normally chemicals such as chlorine bleach mixed with a thickener. See Bleach. Use vinegar, diluted eucalyptus oil or bicarbonate of soda which will inhibit mould and which are much more pleasant to use (and probably cheaper).

NEAT'S FOOT OIL

A very good leather conditioner and protector, produced from the hooves of cows and other similar animals. It is available from hardware stores.

OVEN CLEANERS

If you have left cleaning the oven for too long and the only way to lift off the baked-on grease and dirt is to use a heavy-duty oven cleaner, consider the following when attacking the grime!

Heavy-duty oven cleaners may contain caustic ingredients such as sodium hydroxide, also known as caustic soda. It works on reacting with fats and converting them into water-soluble soapy compounds which can be wiped away.

Non-caustic products, however, contain usual ethanolamine also called monoethanolamine. Another active ingredient is EGEs. These strong chemical cleaners need to be treated with caution. They can have side effects and are harmful to the skin, eyes and lungs. Follow the safety instructions as recommended by the manufacturer.

Ventilate the room before starting the job. Wear protective gloves, long-sleeved clothing, long pants and covered shoes, as well as eye protection and a mask. These will protect your skin, eyes and lungs during use of the product. Avoid inhaling any of the fumes, even it means holding your breath.

Cover the floor with newspaper underneath the oven and surrounding area.

Wipe out the oven with old rags or paper towel and dispose of them in the bin once the job's finished. Always rinse the inside of the oven completely with 10% vinegar solution after cleaning. Clean up thoroughly after the task is complete.

PARAFFIN

Used as a cleaning solvent for grease and often found in the manufacture of candles and waxes. It is a hydrocarbon found in natural gas and petroleum. It is sold in various forms and can be used to clean off rust from bicycle and motor car parts.

PETROLEUM JELLY

This semi-solid form of mineral oil (see Paraffin) can be used as a lubricant to assist in removing any stubborn stains.

PERCHLORETHYLENE

A dry-cleaning solvent which is non-flammable and now used by 85 per cent of professional drycleaners. Like other dry-cleaning fluids, use with caution. Always use in a well-ventilated room for spot dry-cleaning or use alternative spot cleaning methods (see Dry-cleaning fluid).

PHENOL (CARBOLIC ACID)

A strong disinfectant, often an ingredient in disinfectant compounds. It is a benzene derivative found in coal tar. It will kill helpful bacteria in septic tanks and it also will kill some plants. It is not recommended for general household use as there are less toxic disinfectants available. (Creosol is a very similar product and used as a wood preservative, disinfectant and cleaner.)

PRE-WASH CLEANERS

These can be bars of soap-like solvents, or spray-on cleaners. They contain a variety of chemical ingredients such as sodium percarbonate, 'hard' surfactants, perfumes, water softeners, hydrogen peroxide, enzymes and solvents. Use soap-based pre-wash products or soak in ordinary laundry detergent where possible.

ROUGE (JEWELLERS' ROUGE)

A red powder made from ferric oxide used for cleaning and polishing precious metals and gemstones.

RUST REMOVERS AND INHIBITORS

There are quite a few products which come into this category. They can be painted or sprayed on to surfaces to prevent rust like a sealer. Some are rust converters which form a protective coating. Most of them contain phosphoric acid, corrosives, oxalic acid and solvents. Be aware which metals if not properly cared for will rust and take steps to protect them accordingly.

SADDLE SOAP

A soap and not a detergent which is specially designed for cleaning leather. It is very effective for cleaning polished leathers. Always apply a leather conditioner after using the soap.

SCOURING CLEANING POWDERS

These products usually contain bleaches, silver sand, pumice, or whitening and perfumes. They are probably too rough for most household surfaces and will scratch enamel finishes, bathroom and kitchen fittings and sinks. The most common use is to remove soap scum off baths and showers so try using less harmful and less scratchy cleaners.

SOAP

Before detergent there was soap! Nowadays we can still buy laundry soap, soap flakes and of course personal soap. Soap is made from animal fat or vegetable oils with the addition of caustic soda. In some laundry products there may be additions such as borax, bleach, sodium phosphates and perfumes. Soap does not dissolve in cold water so if you use it as a laundry product dissolve it first in hot water. Never use laundry soap as a personal soap because the additives could cause skin and respiratory problems. Soap is a more natural alternative to detergents. Be aware that some liquid 'soaps' are usually made from synthetic detergents.

SODIUM CARBONATE *see* WASHING SODA

SUGAR SOAP

This a strong corrosive synthetic detergent which contains an alkaline chemical and surfactants. It is used to clean grease and grime from most household surfaces, especially walls, before they are to be painted, and it also removes mould.

SWIMMING POOL AND SPA TREATMENTS

Used to control the growth of bacteria and algae in the water, these products may have different strength and application methods. Consult your pool shop for instructions on use in your pool if you are not sure (see the section on outside areas in chapter 4). Most treatments contain chlorine and care should be taken when using any of the treatments.

TEA-TREE OIL

A powerful antiseptic oil similar to eucalyptus oil. It can be used as a disinfectant for kitchens and bathrooms. It can be purchased from healthfood stores, hardware stores and supermarkets. Use in diluted form, a few drops added to a litre of water.

TOILET CLEANERS

There are several products to choose from—powders, liquids and tank clip-on flush dispensers. Some products will clean, deodorise and disinfect, and contain odour-hiding perfumes. They can contain bleach, detergents and paradichlorobenzene (a deodoriser and disinfectant). Never mix toilet cleaners with other household chemicals as a dangerous gas will form. Toilet cleaners can cause problems with the bacteria balance in our waterways. Use less harmful cleaners, and regularly use a toilet brush and cloth to clean with vinegar and very hot water which will kill bacteria.

TURPENTINE AND MINERAL TURPENTINE

Turpentine is made from balsam extracted from conifers. It is highly aromatic and used to assist in the drying process of oil paints. Mineral turpentine (turps) is a petroleum-derived solvent with added benzene-type components. Both can be found in oil-based house paints and are used as thinning agents for paint, lacquer and varnish. They can also be used as solvents for stain removal.

TYPEWRITER CORRECTION FLUID

Usually made from trichloroethane which is a strong grease stain remover. There are less toxic correction fluids which are water-based as well as correction papers and tapes.

VINEGAR (ACETIC ACID)

White vinegar is used as a very efficient household cleaner and is now sold as one in most supermarkets. Acetic acid is a pure vinegar which is sold through chemists and white vinegar is the diluted form which includes some impurities. Generally white vinegar is successful in carrying out a variety of household cleaning tasks. It should not be used on acetate fabrics as it may dissolve the surface.

WASHING SODA (SODIUM CARBONATE)

This can be bought in either crystal or powder form. It is a mild alkali which can be used as an effective stain remover. It is made from sodium carbonate which is used as a water softener in some detergents and will assist with laundry tasks when used in conjunction with pure soap. It also can be used as a tarnish remover for silver and will help unblock drains. It should not be used on silks, woollens or vinyl.

Washing soda (sodium carbonate) can irritate the skin, so wear protective gloves when working with it. Diluted in water, and combined with a little elbow grease, it can be an effective grease remover when used with steel wool.

WATER SOFTENERS

In areas where there may be a problem from hard water, softeners are a useful additive. Low suds with washing-up liquids or powder can be solved by using a water softener which increases the efficiency of the detergent. Washing soda or borax works quite well as an alternative.

WAX (SHOE, CAR, FURNITURE, LEATHER AND FLOOR POLISH)

Natural waxes are made from plants or animals and are usually hard and non-greasy. They do not leave grease marks on paper and they are used to polish and protect furniture, floors, leather and shoes as well as cars. Synthetic wax is also used to protect and to waterproof. Wax can come in a cream or liquid form as well as a paste. Cream and liquid wax usually contain emulsifiers and silicones to help them spread more easily and also make them waterproof. White spirit is usually added to wax pastes to assist in the application and as it dries the white spirit will evaporate leaving a thin coating of wax.

WHITE SPIRIT

Similar to mineral turpentine and acts as a grease solvent. Use as directed for stain removal, but try vinegar or lemon juice as a grease solvent instead where possible.

WINDOW CLEANERS

Similar in content to an all-purpose spray cleaner and may contain ammonia, solvents and detergents.

Chapter 9

RECIPES FOR
HOMEMADE CLEANING PRODUCTS

These cleaning recipes are simple to prepare, easy to use, inexpensive—and you'll know what is in them!

When preparing recipes for household cleaning products make sure you have read the recipe and have all the ingredients and equipment you need together before you start. This makes it easier and quicker to follow these recipes.

You may need:

- a clean plastic laundry bucket with a lid for mixing
- measuring spoons, scales and cup measures
- a grater or an electric food processor (which makes grating soap easier)
- an electric or hand-held whisk for mixing ingredients. An electric blender may also be useful.
- a stainless steel saucepan if blending corrosive materials, mixing or melting ingredients
- a double-boiler for melting ingredients like beeswax
- old bottles and plastic containers. These make excellent storage containers.

Clearly label every cleaner you produce and make sure they are stored out of the reach of children in a safe place.

All of the ingredients are readily available from supermarkets, hardware stores or healthfood or artist supply stores.

All-purpose floor cleaner

1 cup of basic household soap cleaner or 4 tbsp of pure soap flakes
melted in 1 cup of hot water
2 cups vinegar
3 tsp eucalyptus oil or tea-tree oil
8 L of hot water

Method

Mix together in a bucket and apply with a cotton or squeegee mop.
Rinse with warm clean water. Suitable for sealed cork, vinyl, linoleum,
sealed timber floors, terrazzo, glazed ceramic and quarry tiles and
slate.

All-purpose furniture cleaner

25 mL light olive oil
1 cup white vinegar

Method

Mix well together and store in a water spray bottle. Spray onto
furniture then wipe over with a damp cloth and finish drying with a
clean lint-free cloth.

Basic household soap cleaner

This recipe makes about 20 litres
100 g pure soap
1 cup washing soda
1 cup white vinegar
3 tsp eucalyptus oil or tea-tree oil
a few drops of lemon or lavender pure essential oil to add some
perfume
10 L cold water
9 L hot water

Method

Grate the soap and place into a large saucepan and cover with 2 L of
cold water. Bring to boil and then add the washing soda crystals and
stir until completely melted. Stir in the eucalyptus oil, vinegar and the
essential oil. Pour into the bucket and then add in 9 L of hot water and
then stir in 8 L of cold water. Leave to cool. When cool, transfer to
smaller containers and label.

Use as:

- laundry detergent: suitable for front loading, top loading machines and hand washing, 2–3 cups depending on the load
- pre-soaker for heavily soiled items
- washing-up liquid: use 10–20 mL per 10 L of water
- dishwasher detergent: use 1 cup per load. It will not remove coffee and tea stains from cups.

Brass cleaner

Buttermilk applied to a cloth and then wiped over brass will remove any corrosive marks. Rinse with water and polish with soft dry cloth.

Wash brass in water that had potatoes boiled in it. Afterwards rub in salt and lemon juice, then rinse and polish dry to a shine.

Carpet or upholstery stain-removing foam shampoo

250 mL basic household soap cleaner
400 mL hot water

Method

In a bucket or stainless steel bowl mix the ingredients together and cool. When cool, beat until light and very foamy. Spoon the foam over the stain. Leave for 10 minutes and then wipe over with a damp sponge dipped in white vinegar.

Copper cleaner

Mix equal parts of salt, plain flour and vinegar to a paste. Rub the copper with this mixture until clean. Wash in warm soapy water and buff dry with a soft cloth.

Floor polish stripper

125 mL cloudy ammonia
1 cup basic household soap cleaner or 4 tbsp pure soap flakes
  dissolved in 1 cup boiling water
100 mL methylated spirits
6 L of warm water

Method
Mix all the ingredients in a large bucket. Apply to the floor with a sponge mop and allow the stripper to soak into the wax for a few minutes. Scrub with a soft long-handled brush and then sponge mop with clean warm water to remove any residue. Allow to dry thoroughly before applying wax polish. Do a small area at a time.

Floor wax polish

75 g beeswax
250 mL basic household soap cleaner or 4 tbsp of pure soap flakes
  dissolved in 1 cup of boiling water
500 mL raw linseed oil
1 tsp tea-tree oil
500 mL pure turpentine

Method
In a double-boiler heat the beeswax until melted and stir in the household soap cleaner. Remove from the heat and cool. When cool beat in the raw linseed oil, tea-tree oil and pure turpentine. Mix until it is a thick creamy liquid. Pour into an airtight container. Apply to floors with a soft cloth or rag mop. Buff up while still damp with a rag mop or electric floor buffing machine.

Furniture cleaner

50 mL boiled linseed oil
25 mL natural turpentine
25 mL water
2 drops lemon pure essential oil

Method
Mix together in a clean glass bottle. Apply with a clean soft cloth and then wipe over with a soft lint-free cloth.
  Use to clean and polish wooden furniture.

Furniture cream

125 mL water
2 tbsp pure soap flakes
125 g natural beeswax
2 cups pure turpentine
2–3 drops lemon pure essential oil

Method

Put the water in a saucepan, add the soap flakes and heat over a low flame. When dissolved set aside to cool. Melt the beeswax in a double saucepan over boiling water. Remove from the heat and beat in the water and soap flake mixture. Cool a little before blending in the turpentine. Beat together until smooth. Pour into a wide-mouthed jar or container and cover with an airtight lid.

Use on sealed or polished wood furniture. Apply with a soft lint-free cloth. Polish afterwards with a soft, dry, lint-free cloth.

Household spray-and-wipe cleaner

4 L hot water
2 tbsp cloudy ammonia
125 mL white vinegar
2 tbsp bicarbonate of soda
2–3 drops lavender or lemon oil
2 tbsp basic household soap cleaner

Method

Pour 4 litres of hot water into a bucket and mix in all the ingredients. Let cool and pour into water spray bottles.

Use as an all-purpose cleaner for kitchens and bathrooms surfaces.

Silver cleaner

Wash as for brass in potato water. Rinse and then polish dry. Whiting (finely ground chalk, available from hardware stores) mixed with methylated spirits to a paste can be applied to silver and then gently rubbed off with a soft cloth. Wash in hot water and then polish with a soft dry cloth.

Wall and paint cleaner

1 L hot water
1/4 cup washing soda crystals
4 L cold water
125 mL cloudy ammonia
125 mL white vinegar

Method

Mix the hot water and washing soda crystals together and place in a large bucket. Pour in about 4 L of cold water and add the rest of the ingredients. Apply with a sponge and rinse with a clean water with a sponge.

Window, mirror and glass cleaner

6 L water
50 mL cloudy ammonia
1 tbsp basic household soap cleaner or pure soap flakes dissolved in the 6 L of water
1 cup methylated spirits

Method

Mix all the ingredients into a bucket. Pour into a water spray bottle and spray onto dirty surface. Wipe over with a damp sponge and polish dry with a damp chamois cloth. Use on very dirty greasy windows.

USEFUL ADDRESSES

Aerosol Association of Australia Inc
PO Box 1300
Parramatta NSW 2124
Phone (02) 9633 9011
Fax (02) 9635 3284
www.aerosol.com.au

Australian Association for Environment Education
PO Box 4205
University of Melbourne
Parkville VIC 3052
Phone (03) 8344 9807
www.olt.qut.edu.au/udf/aaee

Australian Conservation Foundation
Head Office
Floor 1
60 Leicester St
Carlton VIC 3053
Phone (03) 9345 1111
Fax (03) 9345 1166
www.acfonline.org.au

Sydney
Level 1
29–35 Shepherd Street
Chippendale NSW 2008
Phone (02) 9212 6600
Fax (02) 9212 6977

Canberra
PO Box 2699
Canberra City ACT 2601
Phone (02) 6247 2472
Fax (02) 6247 5779

Adelaide
120 Wakefield St
Adelaide SA 5000
Phone (08) 8232 2566
Fax (08) 8232 2490

Cairns
Ground Floor
130 Grafton St
Cairns QLD 4870
Phone (07) 4051 3892 or
(07) 4051 3326
Fax (07) 4041 4535

Australian Consumers' Association
57 Carrington Road
Marrickville NSW 2204
Phone (02) 9577 3399
Fax (02) 9577 3377
www.choice.com.au

Australian Greenhouse Office
John Gorton Building
GPO Box 621
Canberra ACT 2601
Phone (02) 6274 1888
www.greenhouse.gov.au

Clean Up Australia Ltd
www.cleanup.com.au

Greenpeace Australia Pacific
Level 4
35-39 Liverpool St
Sydney NSW 2000
Phone (02) 9261 4666
www.greenpeace.org.au

Planet Ark Environmental Foundation
www.planetark.com
www.recyclingnearyou.com.au

Plastics and Chemicals Industries Association
Level 2
263 Mary Street
Richmond VIC 3121
PO Box 211
Richmond VIC 3121
Phone (03) 9429 0670
Fax (03) 9429 0690
www.pacia.org.au

Standards Australia
Head Office
SAI Global Limited
286 Sussex Street (cnr Bathurst Street)
Sydney NSW 2000
GPO Box 5420
Sydney NSW 2001
Phone (02) 8206 6000
Fax (02) 8206 6001
www.standards.com.au
Offices in most capital cities

Total Environment Centre
Level 2
362 Kent Street
Sydney NSW 2000
Phone (02) 9299 5599 or
(02) 9299 5680
Fax (02) 9299 4411
www.tec.nccnsw.org.au

Water conservation information sites
www.savewater.com.au.
www.conservewater.melbournewater.com.au
www.sydneywater.com.au
www.watercare.sa.gov.au
www.water.act.gov.au
www.wrc.wa.gov.au

The Wilderness Society
National Office
57E Brisbane Street
Hobart TAS 7000
GPO Box 716
Hobart TAS 7001
Phone (03) 6270 1701
Fax (03) 6231 6533
www.wilderness.org.au

INDEX